MIND-READING

AND

BEYOND

BY

WILLIAM A. HOVEY

BOSTON

LEE AND SHEPARD PUBLISHERS

NEW YORK CHARLES T. DILLINGHAM

1885

BF
1171
H75

ELECTROTYPED BY
C. J. PETERS AND SON, BOSTON.

MIND-READING AND BEYOND.

I.

"FROM the recorded testimony of many competent witnesses, past and present, including observations recently made by scientific men of eminence in various countries, there appears to be, amidst much illusion and deception, an important body of remarkable phenomena which are *prima facie* inexplicable on any generally recognized hypothesis, and which, if incontestibly established, would be of the highest possible value."

This statement is found on the opening page of the first volume of the proceedings of the Society for Psychical Research (London), published in 1882. The Society grew out of a conference held in London, Jan. 6, 1882, and was definitely constituted on the 20th of February following. A programme for future work was at once sketched out by the Council of the Society, in pursuance of which the following subjects were entrusted to special committees : —

I. An examination of the nature and extent of any influence which may be exerted by one mind upon another, apart from any recognized mode of perception.

II. The study of hypnotism, and the forms of so-called mesmeric trance, with its alleged insensibility to pain; clairvoyance, and other allied phenomena.

III. A critical revision of Reichenbach's researches with certain organizations called "sensitive," and an inquiry whether such organizations possess any power of perception beyond a highly exalted sensibility of the recognized sensory organs.

IV. A careful investigation of any reports, resting on strong testimony, regarding apparitions at the moment of death, or otherwise, or regarding disturbances in houses reputed to be haunted.

V. An inquiry into the various physical phenomena commonly called Spiritual; with an attempt to discover their causes and general laws.

VI. The collection and collation of existing materials bearing on the history of these subjects.

The Society declared that it was its aim to approach these various problems "without prejudice or prepossession of any kind, and in the same spirit of exact and unimpassioned inquiry which has enabled science to solve so many problems, once not less obscure, nor less hotly debated."

Considering the nature and scope of the work undertaken by this Society, it becomes interesting to know who compose it and who are its leading spirits. Professor Henry Sidgwick, of Trinity College, Cambridge, is President. There are a number of Vice Presidents; among them, Professor W. F. Barrett, F.R.S.E., of the Royal College of Science, Dublin; the Bishop of Carlisle; Professor Lord Rayleigh, F.R.S., of Cambridge; and Professor Balfour Stewart, F.R.S., of the Owens College, Manchester. The Honorary Members are Professor J. C. Adams, LL.D., F.R.S., of the Cambridge (England) Observatory; Professor Ruskin, LL.D., D.C.L.; William Crookes, F.R.S.; Lord (Alfred) Tennyson; Alfred Russell Wallace, F.R.G.S.; and G. F. Watts, R.A. Nicholas M. Butler, of Columbia College, New York, and Rev. Dr. E. P. Thwing, of Brooklyn, are named among the Corresponding Members. The list of members includes four hundred names, in which the learned professions are very largely represented, the nobility by no means infrequent, and the gentry abundant. An examination of this list will convince any one at all familiar with the names of people prominent in science, in law, in the church, in medicine, in the army, in literature, or in any other leading walk in life in England, that this Society is made up of, and controlled by, as much genuine scientific ability and integrity as any learned body in the kingdom. It seems necessary to dwell upon this fact, because, in America, the investigation of these alleged phenomena has, so far as the public has been aware, been in the hands of persons utterly unfitted for scientific research, the greater number of them ignorant enthusiasts, and not a few practising deliberate swindling for purposes of gain. In England the work seems to have fallen into hands which may fairly be presumed to be competent, and which certainly are honest; and its results possess a value with which that of the desultory, fragmentary, and wholly disconnected efforts put forth in this country bear no comparison.

In his address at the first general meeting of the Society, Professor Sidgwick,[1] the President, noting the fact that some question had been raised as to the need of such an organization, gave expression to an idea that must have occurred to many, although no one had, perhaps, previously reduced it to exact form. He declared it to be nothing less than a "scandal" that the dispute as to the reality of these alleged phenomena should still be going on, that so many competent witnesses should have declared their belief in them, that so many should be profoundly interested in having the question determined, and yet, that the educated world, as a body, should still be in the attitude of incredulity. And he went on to say that the true aim of the Society was and should be to remove this scandal in one way or another, to get at the actual facts, and make them known to the world. That this should be the aim of all honest investigation, scientific or otherwise, will not be questioned. It cannot concern itself with results until they are attained. Its conclusions derive their value from the fact that they cannot be foreseen by the investigators. The great object is to get at the Truth, and certainly Truth is something which no one need be ashamed to seek.

---

[1] From this point on, this opening chapter is practically a compilation of the addresses made by President Sidgwick, at the several meetings of the Society in 1882–84. In many cases his exact words have, in newspaper phrase, been "run in." I have ventured to inject a few ideas and suggestions of my own, but they form an unimportant and trivial part of the whole. The *authorship* of this chapter fairly belongs to Professor Sidgwick; my part of the work is simply a matter of selection, arrangement, and connection, — in a word, a piece of editing. — W. A. H.

It was asked at the outset, by persons by no means unfriendly to the work which the Society proposed undertaking, "Why should this attempt succeed more than so many others which have been made during the past thirty years?" To this question, a natural and legitimate one, there are several answers. The first is that the works must and will go on. Investigation will be continued, if not by organized, then by individual effort. The matter is far too important to be left where it now is. Indeed, considering the importance of the questions still in dispute, as compared with other scientific problems on which years of patient and unbroken investigation have been employed, it may be said that no proportionate amount of labor has yet been devoted to these problems. Even were it granted that previous efforts had completely failed, that would still be no adequate reason for not renewing them. But it cannot be admitted that previous efforts have completely failed. The most that can be said is that they have not completely succeeded. Much important evidence has been accumulated, valuable experience has been gained, and very important effects have been produced upon the public mind.

Just here it is in place to make mention of a criticism that was made at the time the Society began its work, a criticism which tended to place its work in a somewhat invidious light. It was assumed that the Society intended to throw aside the results of *all* previous inquiry as untrustworthy, and that the founders arrogated to themselves a superior knowledge of scientific method or intrinsically greater trustworthiness, and that they hoped and expected to be believed, whatever their conclusions might be, although previous inquirers had been uniformly distrusted. The Society makes no such assumption. It does not, it cannot, assume that it can produce evidence better or more reliable than much that has been laid before the public by men of unquestioned scientific repute, but it may justly hope by continued effort to produce much new evidence, and it holds to the opinion that a great deal more evidence is desirable. It may be true that, as some claim, there has long been sufficient evidence to convince reasonable people who have taken pains to consider it ; but it is certainly no less true that the educated world, including many who have given much time and thought to the study of these phenomena, are by no means convinced as yet, and, for this reason, more evidence is wanted. Again, — and this is a point of prime importance, — it is not enough to establish the fact that certain phenomena do occur. That is but a small part of the work. If they do occur, a very impor-tant, an all-important thing, is to ascertain the laws which govern their occurrence. In this way science gets at the subject considered, and forms a groundwork for its study. If we know more of electricity to-day than we did a hundred years ago, it is because thousands of experiments have been tried by competent persons, and from these have been deduced laws which are found to govern and limit the action of this form of force. What electricity is, as expressed in terms commonly understood, we do not know. The same may be said of heat and of light, but, because the existence of electricity, heat, and light are admitted, shall the investigation of phenomena dependent upon them, and the laws which govern them, come to an end ?

Again, it is asked, " If more evidence is required, how much more?" This is a question that cannot be answered in exact terms. The work of accumulating, sifting, and comparing evi-dence must continue until the scientific world is satisfied. Scientific men are, very properly, slow to accept the truth of phenomena which seem to be outside of all known law. It is of the utmost importance that scientific men should demand, in every case, the most rigid proof, and that they should refuse to believe until every reasonable doubt is removed. Of course they may carry this to an unreasonable extreme, and, as a mat-ter of fact, they often do. But even this is better than that they should be too willing to believe, and accept upon insufficient and unreliable evidence. A longer stride than is generally supposed has already been taken. Says Professor Sidgwick, —

" Thirty years ago it was thought that want of scientific cul-ture was an adequate explanation of the vulgar belief in mes-merism and table-turning. Thus, as one man of scientific repute after another came forward with the results of individual investigation, there was quite a ludicrous ingenuity exercised in finding reasons for discrediting his scientific culture. He was said to be an amateur, not a professional ; or a specialist, without adequate generality of view and training; or a mere discoverer, not acquainted with the strict methods of experimental research; or he was not a Fellow of the Royal Society, or, if he was, it was by an unfortunate accident. Or, again, national distrust came in. It was chiefly in America that these things went on ; or, as I was told myself, in Germany, some years ago, it was only in England, or America, or France, or Italy, or Russia, or some half-educated country, but not in the land of *Geist*. Well, these things are changed now ; and though I do not think this kind of argument has quite gone out of use, yet, on the whole, it has been found more difficult to work, and our obstinately incredulous friends, I think, are now generally content to regard the interest that men of undisputed scientific culture take in these phenomena as an unexplained mystery, like the phenomena themselves. Then, again, to turn to a different class of objectors, I think, although I do not wish to overrate the change, that the attitude of the clergy has sensibly altered. A generation ago the investigator of the phenomena of spiritualism was in danger of being assailed by a formidable alliance of scientific orthodoxy and religious orthodoxy; but I think that this alliance is now harder to bring about. Several of the more enlightened clergy and laity who attend to the state of religious evidences have come to feel that the general principles on which incredulous science explains off-hand these modern marvels, are at least equally cogent against the records of ancient miracles, that the two bodies of evidence must, *prima facie*, stand or fall together, or at least must be dealt with by the same methods. Then, again, a generation or two ago we were told to go to the conjuror, and told that we should see that the whole thing was conjuring. I quite think that this direction was, to a great extent, just and important. It is highly desirable that the investigation of these matters should be carried on by men who have tried to acquaint themselves with the performances of conjurors. But we can no longer be told, off-hand, that all the marvels recorded by Mr. Crookes, Professor Zöllner, and others, are easy conjuring tricks, because we have the incontrovertible testimony of conjurors to the contrary. They may be conjuring tricks, but they are, at any rate, tricks which conjurors cannot find out."

For the reasons summarized above, and those given in the extract from Professor Sidgwick's address, it may fairly be said that matters are now more favorable for an impartial reception of the results of careful and thorough investigation, so far as success is had in obtaining positive results, than at any previous time. It is not to be denied that a great amount of evidence has been accumulated to show that a great part of the phenomena generally attributed to spiritual agency are really, in whole or in part, due to fraud or deception of some kind. This is part of the experience which past experiment has furnished, and it is of the utmost importance. But because many counterfeit bank-notes are in circulation, it does not prove that no genuine ones exist. In fact it rather tends to prove that genuine ones *do* exist, and that, for want of the real article, imitations are substituted. And it is partly because the true is mixed with the false, the counterfeit with the genuine, that it is desirable that careful, thorough, and disinterested investigation should be made by competent persons, in order that the wheat may be sifted from the chaff.

"As regards the question of credibility," says Professor Sidgwick, "the important point to bear in mind is that every additional witness who, as Dr. Morgan said, has a fair stock of credit to draw from, is an important gain. Though his credit alone is not likely to suffice for the demand that is made upon it, his draft will help. For we must not expect any decisive result, in the direction at which we primarily aim, on the common sense of mankind, from any single piece of evidence, however complete it has been made. Scientific incredulity has been so long in growing, and has so many and so strong roots, that we shall only kill it, if we are able to kill it at all as regards any of those questions, by burying it alive under a heap of facts. We must keep 'pegging away,' as Lincoln said ; we must accumulate fact upon fact, and add experiment on experiment, and, I should say, not wrangle too much with incredulous outsiders about the conclusiveness of any one, but trust to the mass of evidence for conviction. The highest degree of demonstrative force that we can obtain out of any single record of investigation is, of course, limited by the trustworthiness of the investigator. We have done all that we can do when the critic has nothing left to allege except that the investigator is in the trick. But when he has nothing else left to allege, he will allege that."

It may be taken as the avowed purpose of the Society to bring no evidence before the public that has not been brought to this pitch of cogency. This is proper on many grounds, and one chief ground is this: It is due to the private families or private circles of friends who have allowed the members of the various committees to take part in their experiments, not to leave the subject of the phenomena — when the committee has, by its own methods of investigation, become convinced of the genuineness of the phenomena — to bear alone the injurious suggestions of critics who may find it needful to attack the experiments. The only honorable course open to the Society, in such cases, is to stand strongly by those of whose honesty it is satisfied, and to drive the objector either to admit the phenomena as actual, although inexplicable, at least by him, or to accuse the investigators of lying or cheating, or of a blindness or forgetfulness incompatible with any intellectual condition other than hopeless idiocy.

When the report of the proceedings of the first meeting of the Society was made public, much discussion, public and private, took place. Of course there was a great deal of criticism, the greater part of it beneath notice, because utterly unintelligent. There was more or less unmitigated ridicule, especially in a certain class of highly respectable papers; but, as it is the rule with the press, in England as well as in America, to ridicule that which it does not comprehend, — the London "Times" scorned the idea that the telephone could ever be anything more than an ingenious and interesting toy, — no one paid much attention to it. In the " Pall Mall Gazette," however, appeared an article in a more serious strain. It urged its readers to abstain from inquiring into ghost stories, on account of the dangerous tendency to give them credence, which, on the principles of evolution, must be held to exist in our brains. Owing to the many generations of our ancestors, argued the "Pall Mall," who believed in spirits, we retain in our nervous mechanism "innumerable connections of fibres," which will be developed into superstitious beliefs if we give them the slightest opportunity. Our only chance is to starve these morbid fibres, by steadily refusing them the slightest nutriment in the way of apparent evidence. We must "keep clear of the pitch" of superstition if we would avoid defilement. "The scientific attitude can only be maintained by careful abstention from dangerous trains of thought."

The reply of Professor Sidgwick to this view of the case was forcible and characteristic. At the second general meeting of the Society he said : —

"When I read this article I seemed to remember having heard something like it many years ago, only not quite in the same language, and then it flashed across me that this was the exact counterpart of the dissuasions which certain unwise defenders of religious orthodoxy, a generation ago, used to urge against the examination of the evidences of Christianity. They told us that, owing to the inherited corruption of the human heart, we had a proneness to wrong belief, which could only be resisted by 'steadily neglecting to develop' it ; that we must keep clear of the pitch of free-thinking if we would avoid defilement ; that, in short, the *religious* attitude can only be preserved by careful abstention from dangerous trains of thought. And I remembered the generous and sincere indignation with which our scientific teachers then repudiated these well-meant warnings, as involving disloyalty to the sacred cause of truth, and a degrading distrust of the God-given reason of man ; with what eloquence they urged on us to maintain our privilege of free and unfettered inquiry, to keep our minds impartially open to all evidence from all sources, and follow our reason whithersoever it led, at whatever sacrifice of long cherished conviction ; and I thought how the whirligig of time brings round his revenges, and how the new professor is 'but old priest writ larger' in a brand-new scientific jargon."

Another class of objectors to the investigations were those who were willing to believe that the phenomena had actual existence, but thought it a waste of valuable time for "superior persons" to establish them. They thought the evidence of thought-reading really strong. They saw no reason why there should not be brain waves, or something of that sort. In fact, they had themselves seen and taken part in experiments which seemed to confirm the idea. As for apparitions at the moment of death, they had always believed that there was something in that, but they could not see why educated people should be concerned about it, and, in fact, believed and felt, and felt strongly too, that it would be far better for them to give the time to writing a commentary on Plato, or studying the habits of beetles or earth worms, or in some such way making a really valuable contribution to science or learning. Fortunately for the Society, it did not have to devote time to this objection. Another body of its critics, the incredulous scientists, did not for one moment question the stupendous importance of the conclusions, if only they could believe it possible to establish them, and they admitted that a man would indeed be fortunate who could hope, in any department of recognized science, to light upon a new truth of anything approaching equal importance. So one set of antagonists was set against another, and they were left to fight it out. One believed the phenomena true, but unimportant, while the other believed them untrue, but, *if true*, of the highest possible importance.

Criticism was naturally aroused by the broad range marked out for the Society's work. Some critics, not unfriendly, said that if the investigation had been confined strictly to mind or thought reading, to clairvoyance, and, perhaps, to the different forms of mesmeric sleep, their countenance would not have been withheld, but that, by taking in haunted houses, spirit-rapping, and so forth, the members of the Society really made themselves too absurd. Doubtless, a certain amount of ridicule might have been avoided by limiting the scope of the investigation in some such way, but it could only have been avoided at the expense of consistency. It is to be observed that it does not follow that all these phenomena must stand or fall together, or that proving the phenomenon of thought-reading tends in any way to prove the existence of ghosts. But the Society holds that the general presumption of established science against the possibility of thought-reading, or clairvoyance, is so strong that it could not be much stronger against any other class of alleged facts ; and therefore, if it were judged reasonable to disregard it in the former case on account of the strength of the testimony to actual instances of thought-reading, etc., it would be palpably inconsistent to refuse investigation in other cases in which the quantity and quality of the testimony were such as would be conclusive in any matter of ordinary experience. That the testimony to the so-called haunting of houses was strong enough to establish a case for investigation on this principle, appeared to the Society incontrovertible. Again, it is to be remembered that not a few investigators have been of opinion that very many phenomena alleged to be spiritual, are in reality explainable as growing out of mind-reading, clairvoyance, or mesmerism, and hence it is of the highest importance that actual phenomena, called spiritual, should be critically examined to see whether they can or cannot be shown to have an origin less mysterious than that to which they are ascribed.

It is only just to the Society that its claim to be a truly scientific body, and to carry on its work in a scientific spirit, and by scientific methods, should be understood. Some have urged that this pretension was absurd, on the ground that any success in establishing the truth of the alleged phenomena would be a hard blow for science. Quite the reverse is the fact. It is true that the agreement of experts is the final test of truth, and that, so far as the great majority of experts is concerned, up to the present time, their agreement is not favorable to the truth of the phenomena. But what an eminent statesman said of the political world may, perhaps, be applied to the scientific world — the main duty of a minority is to become a majority, not, perhaps, by antagonism and direct controversy, but by patiently and persistently endeavoring to apply to these obscure matters, methods as analogous as circumstances allow to those by which scientific progress has been made in other departments.

What is meant by "scientific spirit," or rather what the Society means by it, is this: Its aim is to approach the subject without prepossession or prejudice, favorable or unfavorable, "but with a single-minded desire to bring within the realm of orderly and accepted knowledge what appears as a chaos of individual beliefs." In claiming that its methods are scientific, it does not pretend to possess any peculiar or exclusive knowledge or art, needing special elaborate training. "Science," as an eminent naturalist has said, "is only organized common sense;" and on ground so new as that upon which the Society is seeking to advance, the organization of common sense — that is, of scientific method — must necessarily be very rude and tentative. The fact is, that the value to the Society of the eminent scientific experts among its members depends very much less on any technical knowledge or skill in experimentation than on the general habit of mind — the "higher common sense" — which their practice of scientific investigation has given to them; greater readiness and completeness in perceiving considerations and adopting measures which, when once suggested, are not only intelligible, but even obvious, to the common sense of mankind at large.

For instance, nothing can be more obvious than the need of making as systematic and extensive a collection of facts as possible; partly in order to establish as fact what, it is believed, can only be established by such an accumulation of evidence; and partly in order to obtain by classification a general view of the leading characteristics of the facts, so that the work may be started in a right direction for investigating their conditions. But this need does not seem to be thoroughly understood. Thus, a representative of the intelligent public told the Society that it had, after its first year's work, given facts enough, and that the intelligent public demanded a satisfactory theory of them. The "intelligent public" will probably have to restrain its impatience for some little time to come, a restraint which ought not to be difficult, considering the length of time for which it has remained in a state of contented ignorance on these subjects. Again, a person who sent to the President a valuable first-hand narrative of thought-transference at a distance, thought it needful to apologize, on the ground that the Society "must be inundated with these stories." It is in one sense true that the Society was inundated; the stream of them kept and keeps flowing in more strongly than was anticipated; but it desired to be still more inundated, feeling that the tide could not rise too high for its purposes.

It will naturally be understood that, during the course of the experiments, critics were not wanting who stood ready to explain the phenomena by the operation of well-known laws. It is due to the Society to say that every such suggestion, however flippantly made, received due attention, resulting, in some cases, in the adoption of special precautions to avoid the source of error indicated. For instance, before coming to its conclusions as to thought-transference, the Society considered carefully the arguments brought forward for regarding cases of so-called "thought-reading" as due to involuntary indications apprehended through the ordinary senses; and the conclusion was reached that the ordinary experiments, where contact was allowed, could be explained by the hypothesis of unconscious sensibility to involuntary muscular pressure. Hence, special importance was attached to experiments in which contact was excluded; with regard to which this particular hypothesis is clearly out of court.

Again, in the case of Faraday's well-known experiments on table-turning, no doubt Faraday rendered a real public service in preventing ignorant persons from supposing an unknown force required to explain the turning round of a drawing-room table when a group sit down to it at an evening party. And if the eminent physicist had been able to explain in the same simple and effective way the rarer, but yet strongly-attested cases in which tables are reported to have moved without contact, or to have risen altogether off the ground, he would have really "exploded the whole nonsense" of table-lifting. But it is not a scientific way of dealing with a mass of testimony to

explain **what you can, and** say that the rest is untrue; it shows
no "scientific spirit," it is not common honesty.

When a man pays a sum of money to attend a spiritualistic
exhibition in a room over which the recipient of the money has
absolute control, it is reasonable to attribute to preparation and
sleight-of-hand whatever of the results could be produced by a
professional conjuror on his platform; but it is not, therefore,
equally probable that similar results in a private dining-room
are due to the hitherto latent conjuring powers of the house-
maid. When a man goes to a house which he believes to be
haunted, it is not a noteworthy fact that he dreams of a ghost; or,
if he lies awake at night in a nervous condition, it is not strange
if he mistake the rattle and sigh of the wind for evidence of
ghostly visitants. But it is not, therefore, proper to class as
"expected" apparitions for which the seers are wholly unpre-
pared, and which they at first take calmly for their relatives.
When a marvellous story is told after dinner by a person who
heard it from a friend of the cousin of the man who was actually
there, we may reasonably suppose that an indefinite amount of
thrilling detail has been introduced in the course of tradition,—
especially if the links in the chain of tradition are supplied by
persons who are not accustomed to regard scientific accuracy as
important in these matters; but it is not, therefore, legitimate to
explain in this way a narrative which is taken direct from the
diary of the original eye-witness. It may ultimately be possible
to show that the whole mass of evidence presented under each of
these heads is clearly explicable by causes which all will admit
to be natural: but this result cannot be attained without a more
careful and patient examination of the evidence than most critics
deem it worth while to give.

For the purpose, then, of the examination undertaken by the
Society, its primary endeavor is to collect phenomena, where
explanations like those above mentioned have at least a high
degree of improbability. In no single case can the admissibility
of such explanations be absolutely excluded, not even in the case
of the Society's most conclusive experiments, when regarded
from the point of view of the outside public. All records of ex-

periments must, as has before been intimated, depend ultimately on the probity and intelligence of the persons recording them, and it is impossible for any investigators to demonstrate to persons who do not know them that they are not idiotically careless or consciously mendacious. They can only hope that, within the limited circle in which they are known, either alternative will be regarded as highly improbable.

The facts concerning the growth of belief in the existence of what is known as the mesmeric state should have weight with those who flippantly deny *in toto* the existence of many of the phenomena which the Society has undertaken to investigate. The mesmeric evidence of a generation ago, which, undoubtedly, failed to satisfy orthodox medical opinion at the time, should be carefully reconsidered. The fact is now universally admitted, that, in the controversy which took place from 1840 to 1850 between the mesmerists and the accredited organs of medical opinion, the latter were undoubtedly, to a great extent, wrong. They repudiated sweepingly an important part of the phenomena reported by the mesmerists, which no instructed person now denies to be genuine. No instructed person now questions the genuine reality of the hypnotic or sleep-waking state as a special abnormal condition of the human organism, in which the hypnotized person is, in a peculiar way, subject to delusions suggested to him from without, and can, in some cases, be made as perfectly insensible to pain as he can by inhaling chloroform or laughing gas. But, at the time named, the "Lancet" and other medical organs refused to admit the genuineness of these phenomena, as decidedly as any of them now refuses to admit the reality of community of sensation. When the most painful surgical operations were successfully performed in a hypnotic state, they said the patients were bribed to sham insensibility, and that it was because they were hardened impostors that they let their legs be cut off and large tumors be cut out without showing a sign even of discomfort. At length this unbelief, in all but the most bigoted partisans, gave way before the triumphant success of Mr. Esdaile's surgical operations under mesmerism in the Calcutta hospital, and hence, when subsequently a German professor [Heidenhaim] reported that he had obtained results similar to Braid's, — which had been previously neglected, — orthodox medical science willingly allowed the hypnotic state to take a recognized place in physiological works. The existence, indeed, of a peculiar *rapport* between the mesmeriser and his patient — such as the transference of sensation manifests, — has still the weight of medical authority against it; but this weight is surely diminished by the fact that it was so long and obstinately thrown into the wrong scale as regards the hypnotic state generally.

It is claimed by many that persons who expect to induce a belief in these peculiar phenomena should submit evidence that can be repeated at will; that they must refuse to entertain the idea of " rare, fitful, and delicate " phenomena which cannot be reproduced at will in the presence of any number of skeptics. But there has not been any serious attempt to justify this refusal on general principles of scientific method. The phenomenon of thought-transference — assuming it to be genuine — depends, *prima facie*, on the establishment of a certain relation between the nervous systems of two persons; and as the conditions of this relation are specifically unknown, it is to be expected that they should be sometimes present and sometimes absent, in some unexplained way; and, in particular, it is to be expected that this peculiar function of the brain should be easily disturbed by mental anxiety or discomfort of any kind.

II.

FOR several years prior to submitting their first report to the Society, July 17, 1882, the members of the committee on what is variously called mind-reading, thought-reading, or thought transference, had been gathering evidence on the obscure but important question of *supersensuous sensation.* Stray facts, met with from time to time in the course of their observations, or related to them by competent witnesses, led them to doubt the sufficiency of the popular physiological explanations to account for all cases, and encouraged them to persevere in an inquiry which they stated in the following form : —

Is there, or is there not, any existing or attainable evidence, that can stand physiological criticism, to support a belief that a vivid impression or a distinct idea in one mind can be communicated to another mind without the intervening help of the recognized organs of sensation. And if such evidence be found, is the impression derived from a rare or partially developed and hitherto unrecognized sensory organ, or has the mental precept been evoked directly, without any antecedent sense percept. The *nature* and the *laws* of this direct action of mind on mind would, of course, form a subject of prolonged subsequent discussion and inquiry whenever the evidence in its favor had accumulated sufficiently. The committee says : —

The present state of scientific opinion throughout the world is not only hostile to any belief in the possibility of transmitting a single mental concept, except through the ordinary channels of sensation, but, generally speaking, it is hostile even to any inquiry upon the matter. Every leading physiologist and psychologist down to the present time, has relegated what, for want of a better term, has been called thought-reading, to the limbo of exploded fallacies. Dr. W. B. Carpenter, whose name and distinguished contributions to the science and literature of physiology command universal recognition and respect, finds in the so-called thought-reading a striking confirmation of views he has long advocated, that the "communications are made by unconscious muscular action on the part of one person, and automatically interpreted by the other." Where collusion does not come into play, all that Dr. Carpenter has ever seen or heard rests upon the "intermediation of those expressional signs which are *made* and *interpreted* alike unconsciously." Dr. H. Maudsley, in his "Pathology of Mind," takes the same view as Dr. Carpenter, treating the subject as hardly worthy of serious refutation. Collusion, hallucination, unconscious interpretation of unconsciously imparted signs, furnish, according to the physiologists of to-day, abundant explanation of the phenomena under investigation.

Twelve months ago, the performances of Mr. Irving Bishop having attracted considerable attention, a small committee of distinguished men investigated the matter, and after a few and rather hastily conducted experiments, a report, approved of by the other members of the committee, was drawn up by Mr. G. J. Romanes, and published in "Nature" for June 23, 1881. The report indicates that one member of the committee, Professor Ray Lankester, absolutely refused to countenance the idea of thought-reading, and objected to the other members — Professor Croom Robertson, Mr. F. Galton, and Mr. Romanes — giving even a fair trial to "so puerile a hypothesis." The trial was, however, made, and the result is thus stated: "From these experiments, it is needless to say, we did not anticipate any results; but, with the exception of Professor Lankester, we thought it worth while to make them, not only because Mr. Bishop seemed to desire it, but also to satisfy the general public that we had given the hypothesis of 'thought-reading,' as well as that of 'muscle-reading,' a fair trial."

Mr. Stuart Cumberland has obtained considerable notoriety by experiments somewhat similar to those of Mr. Bishop, but his performances have no sort of relationship to our experiments, as he expressly disclaims thought-reading, and denies the possibility of obtaining any results without contact. Mr. Bishop, on the other hand, professes to obtain results without contact, but the experiments for which he makes this claim are never obtained without the very closest proximity, nor without accompaniments of needless flurry and excited pantomime, which are eminently calculated to distract and mislead the attention.

Mr. Bishop's and Mr. Stuart Cumberland's performances are in some respects identical with those exhibited, some years past, by a Mr. Corey, and others, in America. In a paper read before a scientific body in Detroit, and published in the *Detroit Review of Medicine* for August, 1875, Dr. T. A. McGraw describes as follows the method followed by Mr. Corey in his experiments: "Bringing himself," says Dr. McGraw, "into direct physical contact with some person, Mr. Corey was enabled to discover objects which that person had secreted, and to select from a multitude of objects the one upon which the willer was intent. All his performances were but variations upon these two strings. A hidden object was found, or a person, letter, or figure, was picked out from a crowd of others. He usually brought himself into contact with his subject by grasping the subject's hand, and applying it to his own forehead, but sometimes placed his own hand also on the brow of his companion." The writer proceeds to show that Mr. Corey's tests (like most of those of Mr. Bishop and Mr. Cumberland) are only ideas which can be expressed by the simplest kind of *action*. "He cannot detect any kind of an idea in such a way as to express it first by speech. Thus he cannot tell directly the date of a coin, nor can he discover it in any other manner than by choosing out the figures which represent it from among others on a table." It is obvious, as the writer goes on to say, that most of the actions "could be explained by the perception, by a trained operator, of involuntary and unconscious muscular movements."

"I myself," he continues, "experienced this tendency to involuntary action, when trying to carry out fairly one of Mr. Corey's tests. The object of the search in this case was the date of an old coin, and the operator was trying to discover it by choosing from among the figures on the table those of the proper date. While keeping my attention fixed on a certain figure, I became all at once aware that I was actually trying to force the hand of my associate towards it, so powerfully did the thought impel to the correspondent action."

Notwithstanding this, Dr. McGraw does not believe the explanation he has just given covers *all* the phenomena he witnessed, for he adds: "It seemed to me that there were features in these exhibitions which could not be satisfactorily explained on the hypothesis of involuntary muscular action, for . . . we are required to believe a man could unwillingly, and in spite of himself, give information by unconscious and involuntary signs that he could not give under the same circumstances by voluntary and conscious action. . . . It seems to me there is a hint towards the possibility of the nervous system of one individual being used by the active will of another to accomplish certain simple motions. There would be nothing inherently impossible in this when we recollect the strong similarities that exist between nervous and electrical forces; and as we know, it is possible to generate induced currents of electricity in coils of wire that are near to a primary electric coil; so we can imagine the nervous current to be continued into [induced in?] another body, and act there upon the automatic centres of action. . . . The whole matter, however, needs as yet the most careful investigation before the phenomena can even be accepted as genuine."

Dr. Beard, of New York, professes to have supplied this need, and in various papers — on "Trance," on the "Scientific Basis of Delusion," on the "Physiology of Mind Reading," etc., — published in the American "Popular Science Monthly" for 1876, 1877, and 1879, has, according to the high authority of Professor Croom Robertson (*Nature*, July 14, 1881), "given a varied record of facts, and a series of carefully drawn conclusions." We have carefully read what Dr. Beard has written, and failed to find much more than a singular exhibition of self-assertiveness; coupled with a marked disregard of many eminent names in the past and present records of scientific inquiry. Dr. Beard tells us that after incredible labor he has discovered six sources of error, open to all who experiment with living human beings. "All of these errors are to be recognized, and systematically, and, if possible, simultaneously guarded against, if our results are to command the confidence and homage of science."

These six sources of error are as follows : —

1. *The phenomena of the involuntary life in both the experimenter and the subject,* — embracing under this head trance, as well as all actions below the plane of consciousness.

2. *Unconscious deception on the part of the subject experimented on,* which appears to be a particular instance of the general statement given in the first error.

3. *Intentional deception on the part of the subject;* experiments must be made without any regard to the moral character of the subject.

4. *Unintentional collusion of third parties,* — meaning, by this, bystanders or assistants, seen or unseen; to avoid this, the experiments must be made privately, or the audience kept absolutely silent.

5. *Intentional collusion of third parties, i. e.,* assistance designedly given; difficult to guard against, for, as Dr. Beard remarks, intentional and deliberate deception is more common among the better classes than is generally imagined.

6. *Chance and coincidences.* Concerning this last, Dr. Beard remarks that the only way to eliminate this error is by making comparative experiments with all the sources of error removed except chance. "In this way," he continues, "it was shown that mind-reading, so-called, was really muscle-reading. In the researches I made on muscle-reading, it was shown over and over that by pure chance only the blindfold subject would, under certain conditions, find the object looked for in one case, and sometimes in two cases, out of twelve."

The first two sources of error are considered the most frequent and fatal, and, to guard effectively against them, "two, and only two, things are considered needful : one is a general knowledge of the phenomena of the involuntary life, and the other is so to deceive the subject experimented on that this involuntary action of his mind or body cannot come in and destroy the experiment."

But may not the experimenter himself be deceived by his

foregone conclusions ?   In fact, we venture to think Dr. Beard and others have omitted one source of error more fatal to accuracy in interpreting the results obtained than perhaps any other.   We allude to the strong prepossessions with which the subject is approached, a prejudice which concludes against their possibility, and which, if it does not preclude inquiry, destroys all calmness and impartiality in viewing the facts.   It is undeniable that a strong mental bias in one direction is as objectionable on the side of skepticism as on the side of credulity.   In either case it tends (1) to explain the facts in accordance with the mental bias, which may be erroneous; (2) to produce an actual mental disturbance, either perceptible or imperceptible, which in delicate mental operations may really be as fatal to their success as slight air disturbances in the indications of a galvanometer, or the introduction of a trace of a magnetic metal in the reading of a magnetometer.

Hesitation in accepting any facts so novel, and, in many ways, suspicious, as mind-reading, is, of course, perfectly justifiable; and we are quite prepared to expect much criticism and prolonged experiment, before any generalization from the facts can meet with wide acceptance.   Our own researches have now extended over a period of several years, and we have witnessed phenomena of more or less interest in a great variety of subjects. Broadly speaking, these phenomena may be grouped under the following heads : —

I. Where some action is performed, the hands of the operator being in gentle contact with the subject of the experiment.

II. Where a similar result is obtained with the hands *not* in contact.

III. Where a number, name, word, or card has been guessed and expressed in speech or writing, without contact, and apparently without the possibility of the transmission of the idea by the ordinary channels of sensation.

IV. Where similar thoughts have simultaneously occurred, or impressions been made, in minds far apart.

I. Whenever the hands are in contact, or even communicate

by a tense cord with the subject of the experiment, it is almost impossible to exclude giving faint indications to the guesser, which with a sensitive subject are interpreted into a sense of rightness or wrongness that ultimately may lead them to the hidden object, "the communication," as Dr. Carpenter remarks, "being made by unconscious muscular action on the part of one person and automatically interpreted by the other." The most familiar illustration of this is to be found in the *willing game*, which may be described in Dr. Carpenter's words, as follows: "Several persons being assembled, one of them leaves the room, and during his absence some object is hidden. On the absentee's re-entrance, two persons who know the hiding-place stand, one on either side of him, and establish some personal contact with him, one method being to place one finger on the shoulder, while another is for each to place a hand on his body. He walks about the room between the two 'willers,' and generally succeeds before long in finding the hidden object, being led towards it, as careful observation and experiment have fully proved, by the involuntary muscular action of his unconscious guides, one or the other of them pressing more heavily when the object is on his side, and the finder as involuntarily turning toward that side." [1]

This well-known explanation doubtless accounts for very much that is witnessed in family circles, and which goes under the name of thought-reading. At the same time there is a difficulty in applying it to those cases wherein the subject has frequently failed to accomplish a simple task, and yet has accurately done a much more complicated one, often with singular promptness and decision.

The members of the Committee conducted a series of experiments which come under the first head, that is, with contact between the person "willing" and the person doing the thing "willed." The following is the account of these, as given by Professor W. F. Barrett, Professor of Physics in the Royal College of Science, Dublin: —

[1] Carpenter's "Mesmerism, Spiritualism," etc., p. 54.

The first case is a sample of the ordinary willing game, that came under my notice in Easter, 1877.

Expt. 1.—The subject in this case was a young medical man, and the friends present were mostly medical men, skeptical of the operation of any agency beyond involuntary muscular action. The experiments were made in the house of a distinguished surgeon, Mr. Lawson Tait. A paper-knife was placed by myself on the top of a folding screen, during the subject's absence from the room. On recalling him, two friends clasped hands round the subject's waist; he then closed his eyes, walked irresolutely to the spot, and took off the paper-knife, placing it on the table. Here involuntary guidance to the spot may be assumed, but it is difficult to understand what should have made him lift up his hands, suddenly, and feel for an object out of sight. No indication of what was to be found was given beforehand.

Expt. 2.—The same subject again left the room, one of the number ascertaining that he was quite beyond eye or ear shot. This time we willed that he should move the fire-screen, and double it back. On re-entering, my host, the surgeon, clasped him as before, and after a few moments of indecision he went towards the spot, and did as we had wished.

Expt. 3.—This time we fixed that the subject should turn out the gas of a particular bracket, one of several round the room. Loosely held round the waist, the subject in a few minutes went to the spot, lifted up his hands, and turned off the gas.

These three experiments are of interest, inasmuch as in each one the hands had to be lifted up, muscles being used distant from the part in contact with the willers. Similar results were obtained in July, 1877, with Miss R. as the subject. One example will suffice.

Expt. 4 —During the absence of the subject, it was agreed that a mark should be made with a pencil round a sixpence, which happened to be lying near a sheet of paper, on the table, before the subject left the room. In this case the hands of the willers were placed round Miss R.'s neck, and the action fixed upon silently willed. In a few moments Miss R. walked to the table, took up a pencil, and deliberately made a mark round the sixpence.

A long series of experiments, extending over several days, in May, 1879, were made by me with another subject. In this case the sister of the lady seemed to have the most power over her. Among numerous trials that were made, the following may be quoted.

Expt. 5. — In her absence, the subject was willed to take up a little agate jewel-box, standing with some twenty other small objects on a shelf, put it inside a certain covered jar in another part of the room, reopen the jar, remove the ornament, and hand it to one of the friends present. This was done swiftly and correctly, to the smallest detail.

Expt. 6. — Selected notes on the piano were four times in succession correctly struck. Here, and in Expt. 5, the hands gently touched the head. In some of the next experiments the hands did not actually touch.

Expt. 7. — Certain books, in a bookcase (containing some one hundred volumes), were chosen by me in the absence of the subject. In six consecutive trials the right book was taken down.

Out of a total of one hundred and thirty trials with this subject, of which the foregoing are fair samples, about one hundred were correctly performed. Instead of giving the details of all these experiments, I may be permitted to summarize them by saying that, while in very many cases the muscular sense might have been a sufficient explanation, there were many others very carefully tested, which could not easily be so explained, and which pointed in the direction of something new — such, for example, as mind-reading — as their only satisfactory explanation. In fact, the intervention of a second person, who was entirely ignorant of what had to be done, between the willer and the subject, the hands of each resting on the shoulders of the one in front, did not seriously interfere with the results obtained. Under such conditions difficult things were correctly done, involving complicated muscular actions, whilst we failed to do similar, and even much simpler, things under the influence of deliberate conscious guidance.

Besides these cases, we have received evidence of similar performances in private families in different parts of England, —

at Southampton, Southport, Cirencester, Yarmouth, Cork, Edinburgh, Glasgow, Norwich, etc. In all these cases we are greatly indebted to our informants, to whom we have given considerable trouble in correspondence; but none of these cases were of such a nature as to justify a personal visit, and, moreover, the hypothesis of muscle-reading might, *primâ facie*, be taken to account for many of them. Two cases, however, one in London and one on the south coast, seemed deserving of more careful inquiry. In these, as in all the other cases recorded, the subjects freely placed themselves in our hands, a kindness we desire gratefully to acknowledge, regretting the unrequited trouble we have given them.

The case in London — that of Miss C. — has been investigated by each of the members of the committee on thought-reading. Here is the record of four typical experiments, made by Mr. Myers on Nov. 30 and Dec. 7, 1877.

"The mother of the young lady placed three of her fingers, not including the thumb, on the back of Miss C.'s head, the fingers resting apparently quite lightly.

"*Expt.* 1. — I drew on a piece of paper a rough sketch of a house, and showed the sketch to Mrs. C. Miss C.'s head was averted the whole time, no look was interchanged between her and Mrs. C., no other part of their persons was in contact. No one but Mrs. C. saw the drawing. I watched Mrs. C.'s fingers closely, in full gaslight, they seemed to rest lightly on Miss C.'s head; no signals perceptible. The drawing was rudely reproduced, as though by a person drawing in the dark, one of the windows being drawn outside the outline of the house.

"*Expt.* 2. — I wrote a sentence, and showed it to Mrs. C., taking care that Miss C. should not see it. Miss C. then wrote it under the same conditions as above. I chose sentences in foreign languages, that guidance might be less easy.

> *Tu regere imperio.*
> *Se dejò prender.*

These were correctly written.

"*Expt.* 3. — Miss C. then pushed up her sleeve. Mrs. C.

placed three fingers on Miss C.'s arm, above the elbow, and in like manner Miss C. wrote (without having previously seen the words), —

Palma.

This man.

" *Expt.* 4. — The Greek words μεθυ and αναξ were then written, under the same conditions. They were very rudely written, but each letter was distinguishable."

Notwithstanding these surprising results, we were convinced that, granting the hypothesis of involuntary muscular action, and of extreme sensibility on the part of the subject, the probably unconscious, and certainly undiscernible, movements of the touching fingers might possibly serve to convey a sufficient guidance to the girl's delicate skin and responsive organization, even though she might be unaware of her own response.

The other somewhat similar case that reached me was on the south coast, and here also Mr. Myers visited the family and reported as follows : —

NOTES OF EXPERIMENTS WITH THE MISSES B., OCT. 31, 1877.

Miss M. B., henceforward called M.
Miss R. B., „ „ R.

I put my hand on M.'s shoulders. I thought of what I wished her to do, *and told nobody*, except in Experiments 5, 6, 15, and 16.

Expt. 1. — I wished her to take a very small ornament from the chimney-piece — a little china cat an inch high. As soon as my hands were on her shoulders she rushed to the chimney-piece, so quickly that I had difficulty in keeping my hands on her, and instantly picked up the cat, which was inconspicuously placed among many ornaments.

Expt. 2 & 3. — Two failures followed ; she said she felt strong but confused influence.

Expt. 4. — I wished her to go to a book of photographs — one of several in the room — open it, and pause at a certain photograph. She rushed quickly to the book and opened it, but became confused.

Expt. 5. — Mr. B. took one end of a stick, and M. the other. M. took a strap from a table and gave it to a lady at some distance, — the test agreed on while M. was out of the room.

Expt. 6. — A thread was substituted for the stick. M. moved an object previously agreed on — an umbrella in corner of room; but this time after a good deal of hesitation and fumbling.

Expt. 7. — I put my hands on R.'s shoulders and willed her to pick up and eat a biscuit from a plate in corner of room. She at once picked up a biscuit, but did not eat it.

Expt. 8. — I willed her to shake hands with her mother. She rushed to her mother and stroked her hands.

Expt. 9. — I willed her to pick up grape from bunch. She rushed to grapes and picked a few up.

Expt. 10. — I willed her to pick up a hat in distant part of room. The instant my hands touched her she turned sharply round, rushed to the hat, and picked it up.

Expt. 11. — A similar wish failed.

Expt. 12. — I willed her to nod. She stood still and bent her head.

Expt. 13. — I willed her to clap her hands. She did nothing.

Expt. 14. — I willed her to strike on the piano tenth note from right-hand end. She did so after a few seconds' fumbling. As I had opened the piano, she might guess I wished her to go to the piano, but she could not surmise the right note to strike.

Expt. 15. — Eight persons present contributed trifling articles — a half-crown, two pencil-cases, small knife, key, handkerchief, two small purses. These were put in the pocket of a lady present, while R. was out of room. R. re-entered room; M. touched her shoulders. R. rushed to the lady who had the objects, pulled them out one by one, and with shut eyes gave each to its owner — M. withdrawing her hands during part of the process, which was extremely rapid. R. said she did not know to whom she was giving the things; had no sense of connection between the things and the people — merely an impulse to move first one way and then another.

Expt. 16. — I wrote the letters of the alphabet on scraps of paper. I then thought of the word CLARA and showed it to M. behind R.'s back, R. sitting at the table. M. put her hands on R.'s shoulders, and R. with shut eyes picked out the letters C L A R V — taking the V apparently for a second A, which was not in the pack — and laid them in a heap. She did not know, she said, what letters she had selected. No impulse had consciously passed through her mind, only she had felt her hands impelled to pick up certain bits of paper.

This was a good case as *apparently* excluding *pushing*. The scraps were in a confused heap in front of R., who kept still further confusing them, picking them up and letting them drop with great rapidity. M.'s hands remained apparently motionless on R.'s shoulders, and one can hardly conceive that indications could be given by *pressure*, from the rapid and snatching manner in which R. collected the right letters, touching several letters in the course of a second. M., however, told me that it was always necessary that she, M., should *see* the letters which R. was to pick up.

Mr. B. said that M. used at one time to write automatically the thoughts of persons sitting near her — though quite unconscious of what these thoughts were — the hand being moved without any perceptible influence on the brain.

Nov. 1, 1877. — On a second visit similar phenomena occurred, with one new and instructive experiment, viz. : —

Expt. 17. — M. held one end of a stick, and R. the other. I showed M. certain words which I thought of, behind R.'s back; R. then picked out letters, with the hand which was not holding the stick, from a confused pile. She made the words correctly. *When a thread was substituted for the stick she failed to do so.*

Other experiments were subsequently made with this family by two members of our committee. But, marvellous as were some of the things done, nevertheless had we no other case than this to rely upon, I do not think we should be justified in calling in the aid of any new hypothesis to explain the phenomena; in fact, the last experiment shows that in some cases true thought-reading certainly was *not* the cause of the success attained. I may here observe that our President and Mrs. Sidgwick, who made somewhat similar experiments with two other ladies, arrived at the conclusion that all the results witnessed by them personally were capable of explanation by the hypothesis of unconscious perception of unconscious muscular indications. Mrs. Sidgwick writes: "They certainly did very wonderful things, but they did not succeed in any, even very simple, experiments which appeared completely to exclude the muscular hypothesis, except after several attempts. My brother and I both found that with the hands of one of the sisters on our shoulders, we could succeed in doing things fairly well, though slowly; not, however, by feeling any impulse to do anything, but by concentrating our minds on the hands, and trying to make out from them whether their owner was satisfied or dissatisfied. In this way he succeeded, *e. g.*, in selecting the desired card from a number on a table. We found that the close attention necessary for success was assisted by closing the eyes. I should add that I discussed the theory of unconscious muscular action with the Misses X., but they did not think it would account for either their own sensations or some experiments they had succeeded with in their own family circle."

On the other hand it must be admitted that some of the results obtained by Mr. Myers would be far more easily explained by thought-reading, if that were once recognized as a *vera causa*, and the following prior experiments with the same ladies, sent to me by an eye-witness, — whose integrity I have no reason to doubt, — seem quite beyond any power of muscle-reading.

Sept., 1876. *Expt.* 1. — Miss B. seated at the table, with her eyes bandaged, and a pencil in her hand. I stood *behind* her; no word was spoken. I took my spectacles and held them in my hand; she wrote "Spectacles;" then my dog-whistle; after this a key; then a pencil; all these she wrote down correctly.

Expt. 2. — The same young lady, M. B., seated at the table with her eyes bandaged, pencil in hand. Her uncle, standing about twelve feet distance, asked, "What word am I thinking of?" M. B. wrote "Homo." This was right.

Expt. 3. — My daughter, who had recently returned from a visit to her brother at his vicarage, asked M. B. (who was again seated with eyes bandaged, and pencil in hand), " Who preached at my brother's church last Sunday evening ? " the answer to the question being known to my daughter *only.* M. B. wrote the first six letters of the name, viz., " Westmo— " and then said, " I feel no more influence." My daughter said, " Lean your head against me." M. B. did so, and then wrote the rest of the name, making it quite right — " Westmore."

Expt. 4. — My daughter then asked her the following questions : " What is the name of the hotel I was staying at in Paris last month ? " This was answered correctly. " The name of the opera I heard ? " Also answered correctly.

We come now to the second class : *where* ACTIONS *are performed without contact with the person willing.* Under this head the committee say : Here the involuntary guidance by the eyes of the rest of the party, or other indications of an almost imperceptible character, are swiftly and probably unconsciously interpreted by the guesser, and lead him, hesitating, to do what is being willed. The doubtful interpretation of the best results obtained in this group compelled the committee, who were determined never to give the phenomena, as such, the benefit of any doubt, to attach comparatively little importance to them.

The third group covers cases where some number, word, or card, has been guessed apparently without any of the ordinary means of communication between the willer and the guesser. Under this head the committee says : —

Though the errors arising from muscle-reading or involuntary guidance are here avoided, there are other sources of conscious or unconscious illusion to be guarded against. Collusion is one of the most obvious ; and any one who has witnessed what can be done by a code of signals, such as is employed by Mr. Bishop, or Mr. Heller, or Mr. Heriot with " Louie," will naturally distrust all observations where two particular persons are necessary for the results obtained. Imperceptible information may be given by one who knows the words selected, by means of the Morse code used in electric telegraphy, the long and short signs being readily communicated by sight, sound, or touch, as may be found requisite. And where collusion is out of the question, an obvious danger lies in low whispering, or even soundless movement of the lips; whilst the faintest accent of approval or disapproval in question or comment may give a hint as to whether the effort is tending in the right direction, and thus guide to the mark by successive approximations. Any exhibition of the kind before a promiscuous company is nearly sure to be vitiated by one or other of these sources or error. It is obvious, in fact, that precision can only be attained by repeated experimentation in a limited circle of persons known to each other, and amenable to scientific control.

In the correspondence received there was one case which seemed, upon inquiry, to be free from any *primâ facie* objections, and apparently indicative of true thought-reading. It was that of a family in Derbyshire, with whom the committee had the opportunity of frequent and prolonged trials. This family resided in Buxton, and was that of a Mr. Creery, a clergyman of unblemished character, and whose integrity had, it so happened, been exceptionally tested. He had a family of five girls, ranging, at that time (1882), between the ages of ten and seventeen, all thoroughly healthy, as free as possible from morbid or hysterical symptoms, and in manner perfectly simple and child-like. The father's account of the origin and nature of the experiments which were tried in the privacy of his home, as read to the Society for Psychical Research, is as follows:

In the month of October, 1880, my attention was called to the phenomena of the "willing game," but being unable to determine how much of the results was due to simple willing, and how much to involuntary pushing, I resolved to thoroughly investigate the whole question of the action of mind on mind. For this purpose I employed four of my children between the ages of ten and sixteen, all being in perfectly robust health, and a maid-servant, about twenty years of age. Each went out of the room in turn, while I and the others fixed on some object which the absent one was to name on returning to the room.

After a few trials the successes preponderated so much over the failures that we were all convinced there was something very wonderful coming under our notice. Night after night, for several months, we spent an hour or two each evening in varying the conditions of the experiments, and choosing new subjects for thought-transference. We began by selecting the simplest objects in the room; then chose names of towns, names of people, dates, cards out of a pack, lines from different poems, etc.; in fact, any things or series of ideas that those present could keep steadily before their minds; and when the children were in good humor, and excited by the wonderful nature of their successful guessing, they very seldom made a mistake. I have seen seventeen cards, chosen by myself, named right in succession, without any mistake. We soon found that a great deal depended on the steadiness with which the ideas were kept before the minds of "the thinkers," and upon the energy with which they willed the ideas to pass. Our worst experiments before strangers have invariably been when the company was dull and undemonstrative; and we are all convinced that, when mistakes are made, the fault rests, for the most part, with the thinkers, rather than with the thought-readers.

I may say that this faculty is not by any means confined to members of one family; it is much more general than we imagine. To verify this conclusion I invited two of a neighbor's children to join us in our experiments. On the first evening they were rather diffident, and did not succeed; on the second, they improved, and on the third evening they were still better. Circumstances prevented them being able to continue their visits to us, but I saw enough to make me feel perfectly sure that had they persevered they would have been quite equal to our own circle in the faculty of thought-reading.

Those who may be desirous of ascertaining the truth of the matter can do so in their own families; and since it in no way interferes with the health of those engaged, it will be found a very interesting way of passing an hour on a winter's evening.

The distance between the thinkers and the thought-reader is of considerable consequence. As a rule the best results take place when this distance is not more than a yard or two; but, under very favorable mental conditions, we have often had four and five cards named right in succession, while the thought-reader was placed in a room on the landing above that in which the thinkers were assembled.

On questioning the children as to the *mode* by which they form their judgment of the ideas that come before their minds, I find them all agreed in this: two or three ideas of objects of the class with which we are experimenting come before their minds, and, after a few moments' reflection, they select that which stands out with the greatest vividness. At present we are not in a position to theorize very far on this subject, still we cannot help asking ourselves this question: How are the motions of the brains of the thinkers communicated to the brain of the thought-reader? Is there any such thing as direct action between mind and mind? or, are "brain-waves" set up in some intervening medium, either in the luminiferous ether, or in a nerve atmosphere developed at the time in the cerebra of the thinkers, by which the corresponding idea is called up in the mind of the thought-reader? These are questions which, at present, we cannot definitely answer; but I am under the impression that the medium of communication is something more subtle than the vehicle that conveys heat and light.

When we began to investigate these curious phenomena, we had no idea that the result of our little amusement would ever come before the public. But having been asked to deliver a lecture on some popular subject before a small philosophical society in Derby, I volunteered to give an account of the experiments in "thought-reading" with which I was then engaged. A short report, which appeared in the local papers, I forwarded to Professor Barrett, who, I knew, was interested in such matters. He at once took it up, and paid us his first visit at Easter, 1881, the results of which he afterwards published in "Nature;" and should conclusions of any psychological value be ever deduced from the experiments that I commenced, it will be mainly to him that science will be indebted.

Concerning Mr. Creery's family and the experiments with the daughters, the committee say : —

During the year which has elapsed since we first heard of this family, seven visits, mostly of several days' duration, have been paid to the town where they live, by ourselves and several scientific friends, and on these occasions daily experiments have been made.

The inquiry has taken place partly in Mr. Creery's house, and partly in lodgings or in a private room of an hotel, occupied by some of our number. Having selected at random one child, whom we desired to leave the room and wait at some distance, we would choose a card from a pack, or write on paper a number or a name which occurred to us at the moment. Generally, but not always, this was shown to the members of the family present in the room; but no one member was always present, and we were sometimes entirely alone. We then recalled the child, one of us always assuring himself that, when the door was suddenly opened, she was at a considerable distance (in their own house, at the further end of a passage), though this was usually a superfluity of caution, as our habit was to avoid all utterance of what was chosen. Before leaving the room, the child had been informed of the general nature of the test we intended to select, as " this will be a card," or " this will be a name." On re-entering she stood — sometimes turned by us with her face to the wall, oftener with her eyes directed towards the ground, and usually close to us and remote from her family — for a period of silence varying from a few seconds to a minute, till she called out to us some number, card, or whatever it might be. If this was incorrect, we usually allowed a second trial, and occasionally a third.

To give an example : The following results were obtained on the evening of April 12, in the presence of two of our number and the family. The first attempt of one of the children was to state (without searching) the hiding-place of some small object, the place having been chosen by ourselves, with the full range of the house, and then communicated to the other members of the family. This was effected in one case only out of four.

The next attempt was to give the name of some familiar object agreed on in the child's absence, as sponge, pepper-castor, etc. This was successful on a first trial in six cases out of fourteen. We then chose a card from a full pack in the child's absence, and called upon her to name it on her return. This was successful at once in six cases out of thirteen. We then tried holding small objects in the hand, — as a latch-key, a half sovereign, a green ball, — which were at once rightly named in five cases out of six. A harder trial was now introduced. The maid-servant having left the room, one of us wrote down the name "Michael Davitt," showed it round, and then put the paper in his pocket. The door was now opened, and the girl recalled from the end of the passage. She stood close to the door amid absolute silence, and with her eyes on the ground — all of us meanwhile fixing our attention on the appointed name — and gave, after a few seconds, the name "Michael," and then, almost immediately, "Davitt." To avoid any association of ideas, we then chose imaginary names, made up by ourselves at the moment, as "Samuel Morris," "John Thomas Parker," "Phœbe Wilson." The names were given correctly *in toto* at the first trial in five cases out of ten. Three cases were complete failures, and in two the names given bore a strong resemblance to those selected by us, — "Jacob Williams" being given as "Jacob Wild," and "Emily Walker," as "'Enry Walker." It was now getting late, and both we and the younger children were very tired; and four attempts to guess the name of a town in England were all failures, though one of us had previously obtained remarkable success with this very experiment.

The results obtained when the family were present gain enormously in value if similar results can be shown when none but strangers to the family know the word or card selected, or when the child who is the subject of the experiment is completely isolated from those who know the thing chosen. We will therefore describe two series of experiments of this character, which appear to us to be absolutely unexceptionable and conclusive, so far as they go.

Easter, 1881. Present: Mr. and Mrs. Creery and family,

and W. F. Barrett, the narrator. One of the children was sent into an adjoining room, the door of which I saw was closed. On returning to the sitting-room, and closing its door also, I thought of some object in the house, fixed upon at random; writing the name down, I showed it to the family present, the strictest silence being preserved throughout. We then all silently thought of the name of the thing selected. In a few seconds the door of the adjoining room was heard to open, and after a very short interval the child would enter the sitting-room, generally speaking with the object selected. No one was allowed to leave the sitting-room after the object had been fixed upon; no communication with the child was conceivable, as her place was often changed. Further, the only instructions given to the child were to fetch some object in the house that I would fix upon, and, together with the family, silently keep in mind to the exclusion, as far as possible, of all other ideas. In this way I wrote down, among other things, a "hair-brush,"—it was brought; an "orange,"—it was brought; a "wine glass,"—it was brought; "an apple,"—it was brought; a "toasting-fork," failed on the first attempt, a pair of tongs being brought, but on a second trial it was brought. With another child (among other trials not here mentioned), a "cup" was written down by me,—it was brought; a "saucer,"—this was a failure, a plate being brought; no second trial allowed. The child, being told it was a saucer, replied,—"That came into my head, but I hesitated, as I thought it unlikely you would name saucer after cup, as being too easy."

This last trial, some would think, shows pure guesswork, and invalidates the other results; but we prefer to let it stand, as, taken in conjunction with our experience obtained in other ways, it indicates one source of failure; namely, that in delicate experiments of the kind here recorded (assuming them to be cases of thought-transmission), the slightest effort of reason, or of will, on the part of the subject is sufficient to vitiate the success of the experiment. No doubt the chief source of failure is to be found in the difficulty of suppressing the more vivid impressions made on the mind by the ordinary channels of sensation.

We may compare this to the action of a die in stamping; light pressure of the die will yield a delicate and faithful impression, or a blurred and imperfect one, or none at all, according to the nature of the material that is stamped, or the prior existence of any deeply cut impression.

The second series of experiments, which, we venture to think, are unexceptionable, were made by Mr. Myers and Mr. Gurney, together with two ladies who were entire strangers to the family. None of the family knew what we had selected, the type of the thing being told only to the child chosen to guess. The experimenters took every precaution in order that no indication, however slight, should reach the child. She was recalled by one of the experimenters and stood near the door with downcast eyes. In this way the following results were obtained. The thing selected is printed in italics, and the only words spoken during the experiment are put in parentheses : —

Experiments made on April 13, 1882.

Objects to be named.

A white penknife. — Correctly named, with the color, the first trial.

Box of almonds. — Correctly named,

Threepenny piece. — Failed.

Box of chocolate. — Button-box said ; no second trial given.

Penknife hidden. — Failed to name the place.

Numbers to be named.

Five. — Correctly given the first trial.

Fourteen. — Failed.

Thirty-three. — 54 (No).   34 (No).   33 (Right).

Sixty-eight. — 58 (No).   57 (No).   78 (No).

Fictitious names to be guessed.

Martha Billings. — Failed ; Biggis was said.

Catherine Smith. — Catherine Shaw said.

Henry Cowper. — Failed.

Cards to be named.

Two of clubs. — Right first time.

Queen of diamonds. — Right first time.

Four of Spades. — Failed.

Four of hearts. — Right first time.

King of hearts. — Right first time.

Two of diamonds. — Right first time.

Ace of hearts. — Right first time.

Nine of spades. — Right first time.

Five of diamonds. — Four of diamonds (No). Four of hearts (No). Five of diamonds (Right).

Two of spades. — Right first time.

Eight of diamonds. — Ace of diamonds said ; no second trial given.

Three of hearts. — Right first time.

Five of clubs. — Failed.

Ace of spades. — Failed.

The chances against success in the case of any one card are, of course, fifty-one to one, assuming that there is no such thing as thought-reading, and that errors of experiment are avoided. Special precautions were taken to avoid such errors of experiment as are described by Dr. Beard, and the results show that in the case of cards, out of *fourteen* successive trials *nine* were guessed rightly the first time, and only three trials can be said to have been complete failures. On none of these occasions was it even remotely possible for the child to obtain by any ordinary means a knowledge of the card selected. Our own facial expression was the only index open to her; and even if we had not purposely looked as neutral as possible, it is difficult to imagine how we could have unconsciously carried, say, the two of diamonds written on our foreheads.

Now, if we apply to these two sets of experiments the sources of error enumerated by Dr. Beard, the conclusion, we venture to think, is inevitable that we have here very strong evidence in favor of a class of phenomena entirely new to science. *Involuntary actions*, such as movement of the lips, etc., could not reach the child when she was out of sight and hearing, as was the case in the first series of experiments. *Conscious or unconscious deception* on the part of the subject does not apply, as the thing wished for was selected and written down by one of us. *Collusion* by a third party is avoided by the fact that none were allowed to enter or leave the room after we had selected the thing to be guessed, and in the second series of experiments by the exclusion of all members of the family, either from the room, or from participation in the requisite knowledge;[1] whilst *chance and coincidence* we have already dealt with. In many trials, such as the guessing of fictitious names, made up by us on the spur of the moment, the chances against success were, of course, incalculable; yet, as will be seen by the following record taken from our last day's experimenting, these names were guessed with as much ease as cards, where the chances against success were far less.

In the following experiments the thing selected was known to the family, who, however, never left their places after we had written dcwn the word and silently handed it round, or drawn a card, exposed it, and then replaced it in absolute silence. The child was now recalled *by one of us*, and, as before, stood in complete silence near the door, *no sounds nor movements nor interrogatory remarks of any kind by anyone being permitted.* There were present Mr. Gurney and Mr. Myers (Professor Barrett having left the day before) and the family.

Morning of April 17, 1882:
Cards to be named, drawn at random from a full pack. The card selected is printed in italics, the guesses are given in Roman type, and the only remarks made, and those were by us, are put in parentheses.
Five of clubs. — King of hearts (No). Five of clubs (Right).
Two of spades. — Two of spades (Right).
Five of spades. — Four of diamonds (No).

---

[1] In subsequent experiments we obtained successful results by individual trials with each of the children, that is to say, the number, word, or card was known to some *one* of us only.

Three of spades. — Three of hearts (No). Ace of spades (No).

Five of clubs. — Four of clubs (No). Ace of clubs (No).

Two of spades. — Two of clubs (No). Three of clubs (No).

Eight of spades. — Eight of clubs (No). Eight of spades (Right).

Knave of hearts. — Knave of hearts (Right).

Six of hearts. — Six of clubs (No). Seven of clubs (No).

Eight of hearts. — Seven of hearts (No). Seven of clubs (No).

Ace of clubs. — Queen of clubs (No). Ace of clubs (Right).

Two of clubs. — Two of clubs (Right).

Seven of hearts. — Two of diamonds (No). Three of hearts (No).

Two of spades. — Two of clubs (No). Two of spades (Right).

Six of diamonds. — Six of clubs (No). Six of diamonds (Right).

Three of hearts. — Four of hearts (No). Three of hearts (Right).

Eight of diamonds. — Five of diamonds (No). Seven of diamonds (No).

Eight of spades. — Nine of spades (No). Ten of spades (No). Eight of spades (Right).

King of spades. — King of clubs (No). Knave of clubs (No). King of diamonds (No).

Three of spades. — Three of spades (Right).

Knave of diamonds. — King of diamonds (No). Knave of diamonds (Right).

Nine of spades. — Nine of spades (Right).

Ten of clubs. — Ten of hearts (No). Queen of hearts (No).

Three of diamonds. — Three of diamonds (Right).

Six of spades. — Six of spades (Right).

Ten of diamonds. — Ten of diamonds (Right).

Knave of diamonds. — Ace of diamonds (No).

The trials so far were principally with the two children, Maud and Alice ; the eldest sister, Mary, was now tried, with the following results, *every experiment* being given in the order it was made : —

Six of spades. — Eight of clubs (No).   Eight of spades (No).

Ace of diamonds. — Ace of diamonds (Right).

Queen of hearts. — Queen of hearts (Right).

Two of clubs. — Two of clubs (Right).

Ten of spades. — Ten of spades (Right).

Ten of diamonds. — Ten of diamonds (Right).

Five of spades. — Five of spades (Right).

Two of spades. — Two of spades (Right).

Five of diamonds. — Five of diamonds (Right).

Three of clubs. — Four of clubs (No).   Five of clubs (No). Three of clubs (Right).

King of clubs. — Ace of diamonds (No).   Knave of clubs (No). King of clubs (Right).

Five of spades. — Four of spades (No).   Five of spades (Right).

Seven of diamonds. — Five of diamonds (No).   Five of clubs (No).   Seven of diamonds (Right).

Queen of spades. — Queen of spades (Right).

Six of spades. — Six of spades (Right).

Three of spades. — Four of spades (No).   Three of spades (Right).

Knave of diamonds. — Ace of diamonds (No).   Knave of diamonds (Right).

Eight of hearts. — Nine of hearts (No).   Eight of hearts (Right).

Nine of diamonds. — Nine of diamonds (Right).

Knave of clubs. — King of clubs (No).   Knave of clubs (Right).

Four of clubs. — Four of clubs (Right).

Nine of hearts. — Five of hearts (No).   Nine of hearts (Right).

Two of clubs. — Two of clubs (Right).

Six of clubs. — Six of clubs (Right).

King of clubs. — Knave of clubs (No).   King of clubs (Right).

Nine of hearts. — Nine of diamonds (No).   Nine of hearts (Right).

Ten of clubs. — Ten of clubs (Right).

Ace of clubs. — Ace of clubs (Right).

Five of clubs. — Five of clubs (Right).

Seven of clubs. — Five of diamonds (No). Seven of clubs (Right).

Knave of hearts. — Knave of clubs (No). Knave of diamonds (No). Knave of hearts (Right).

Fictitious words were now chosen. During some of these trials Mr. Creery was absent. Miss Mary was the guesser in the first five trials, then Maud was selected; the words chosen are again indicated by italics : —

William Stubbs. — William Stubbs.

Eliza Holmes. — Eliza H——.

Isaac Harding. — Isaac Harding.

Sophia Shaw. — Sophia Shaw.

Hester Willis. — Cassandra, then Hester Wilson.

John Jones. — John Jones.

Timothy Taylor. — Tom, then Timothy Taylor.

Esther Ogle. — Esther Ogle.

Arthur Higgins. — Arthur Higgins.

Alfred Henderson. — Alfred Henderson.

Amy Frogmore. — Amy Freemore. Amy Frogmore.

Albert Snelgrove. — Albert Singrore. Albert Grover.

In estimating our successes and failures, partial success is counted as a failure ; thus, seven of diamonds given instead of eight of diamonds, is counted wrong, and so in the names, — Wilson given instead of Willis, and Grover instead of Snelgrove, are counted as failures.

The outline of results during the present investigation, which extended over six days, stands as follows : — Altogether 382 trials were made. In the case of letters of the alphabet, of cards, and of numbers of two figures, the chances against success on a first trial would naturally be 25 to 1, 51 to 1, and 89 to 1, respectively; in the case of surnames they would of course be indefinitely greater. Cards were most frequently employed, and the odds in their case may be taken as a fair medium sample; according to which, out of the whole series of 382 trials, the average number of successes at the first attempt by an ordinary guesser would be $7\frac{1}{3}$. Of our trials, 127 were successes on the first attempt, 56 on the second, 19 on the third, making 202 in all. On most of the occasions of failure, — 180 in number — second trials were made; but in some cases the guesser professed inability, and declined to make more than one, and in others we allowed three; no trial beyond the third was ever allowed. During the last day or two of trial, after it had occurred to us to notice the point, we found that of the failures to guess a card at the first trial, those wrong both in suit and number were a small minority.

Our most striking piece of success, when the thing selected was divulged to none of the family, was five cards running named correctly on a first trial; the odds against this happening once in our series were considerably over a million to one. We had altogether a good many similar batches, the two longest runs being eight consecutive successes, — once with cards and once with names; where the adverse odds in the former case were over one hundred and forty-two millions to one, and in the latter something incalculably greater. If we add to these results others obtained on previous visits, it seems not too much to say that the hypothesis of mere *coincidence* is practically excluded.

We are aware that the exceptional nature of this inquiry goes far to invalidate arguments founded on character and demeanor; and on this head, therefore, will only state our conviction that any candid critic, present during the whole course of the experiments, would have carried away a far more vivid impression of their genuineness than the bare printed record can possibly convey. Of more real importance is the hypothesis of exalted sensibility of the ordinary sense organs. We could discover no indication of this in any of its known forms; but by way of precaution, as has been already stated, we commonly avoided even whispering any word, number, or name that we had selected; and the position of the excluded child, when the door was opened, would, in every case, have satisfied the most exacting critic. The explanation which might be sought in unconscious indications given by the sitters, and especially in the movement of the lips, has been already adverted to.

Coming, as we did, to this investigation with considerable previous experience of the same kind, we were throughout strictly on our guard against giving such indications ourselves; the possibility of their being given by the family was, of course, excluded where the family were ignorant of the selected word or thing; and on the remaining occasions our perpetual vigilant watch never detected a trace of anything of the kind. The absolute docility of the children — both the guesser and the others — in taking any position in the room that we indicated, was naturally an assistance to our precautions. It may be further mentioned that, on a previous visit made by one of us, the child called the required name through the shut door or from an adjoining room, having thus been completely isolated from the very beginning to the very end of the experiment.

It must be remembered that our great preoccupation throughout was to guard against delusion. Had the phenomena been sufficiently established to allow of a systematic search for their underlying laws, we might have preferred a more unvarying method of experimentation; but in this preliminary stage it seemed desirable to meet *primâ facie* possibilities of deception by frequent and unexpected changes of the various conditions. At the same time we endeavored to gather such indications as we could of the way in which the impression flashed on the mind of the child.

The first question concerns the respective parts in the phenomena played by mental *eye* and mental *ear*. Among the experiments which we have counted as *failures* were very many where the number or card selected was guessed, as it were, piecemeal. For instance, the number 35 was selected, and the guesses were 45 and 43. So 57 was attempted as 47 and 45. So with cards: the seven of diamonds being chosen, the guesses were six of diamonds and seven of hearts; the three of spades being chosen, the guesses were queen of spades and three of diamonds. These cases seem somewhat in favor of mental eye, the similarity in *sound* between three and thirty in 43 and 35, or between five and fifty in 45 and 57, not being extremely strong; while the *picture* of the 3 or the 5 is identical in either pair. A stronger argument on the same side is the frequent guessing of king for knave, and *vice versâ*. On the other hand, names of approximate sound (also reckoned as failures) were often given instead of the true ones; as "Chester" for Leicester, "Biggis" for Billings. Frogmore was guessed first as "Freemore"; Snelgrove was given as "Singrore," the last part of the name was soon given as "Grover," and the attempt was then abandoned; the child remarking afterwards that she thought of "Snail" as the first syllable, but it had seemed to her too ridiculous. One of us has, moreover, successfully obtained from the maid-servant a German word, of which she could have formed no visual image. The children's own account is usually to the effect that they "seem to see" the thing; but this, perhaps, does not come to much, as a known object, however suggested, is sure to be instantly visualized.

Another question would be as to the effect of greater or less distance between the sitters and the guesser, and of the intervention of obstacles. It will have been seen that, in the experiments conducted by one of us on a former occasion, the intervention of a door or wall seemed to make no difference. It would be interesting, again, to discover whether numerical increase in the observers increases the effect, and how far the presence of special persons is influential. In our experience the presence of the father — though by no means essential, and very often dispensed with — seemed decidedly to increase the percentage of successes.

A still more interesting and important question concerns such conditions of success and failure as may lie in the circumstances, disposition, general capacity, and mood of the subject, including such points as consanguinity and familiarity with members of the circle, and also in the temper and manner of the latter. We are dealing, not with chemical substances, but with childish minds, liable to be reduced to shyness and confusion by anything in the aspect or demeanor of visitors which inspires distaste or alarm.

The importance of "a childly way with children," and the slight-
ness of the differences of manner which will either paralyze
them into stupidity or evoke unexpected intelligence and power,
are commonplaces to anyone whose duties have lain among them;
and attention to such points may be as prime a factor of success
in these delicate experiments as any other.

The delicacy of the conditions was illustrated in our own inquiry partly by the inexplicable fluctuations of 'success and failure affecting the whole household, partly by the wide difference
observed in the capacities of particular members of it from day to
day. The common notion that simplicity, and even comparative
blankness of mind, are important conditions, seems somewhat
doubtfully borne out by our experience; but of the favorable
effect of freedom from constraint, and of a spice of pleasurable
excitement, we can speak with entire assurance. The particular ill-success of a sitting which we held one close afternoon
was attributed by the children themselves — and it seemed to us
correctly — to inertness after their early dinner.

We could find no resemblances between these phenomena
and those known as *mesmeric;* inasmuch as a perfectly normal
state on the part of the subject seemed our first prerequisite.
Nor did we find any evidence that "strength of will" has any
particular effect, except so far as both subject and circle may
exercise it in patient attention. On one or two occasions it
seemed of advantage to obtain vivid simultaneous realization of
the desired word on the part of all the sitters; which is most
easily effected if some one slowly and gently claps time, and all
mentally summon up the word with the beats.

Many further lines of the investigation suggest themselves; for
instance, a great step would be made if a more complex idea, and
one not habitually expressed by one definite sound or set of
sounds, could be transmitted. An immense number of accurately recorded experiments will be necessary for the establishment of such special points; and possibly the present instalment
may serve in some degree to stimulate and concentrate various
inquiries in the same direction, which, though widely spread,
seem so far to have been for the most part of a lax and fitful

sort.   The material for such inquiries, as may be surmised from the present record, must be in large proportion children, who are fortunately not rare, and who may be congratulated on so grand an opportunity for combining utility with amusement.

The primary aim in all cases must be to get the results *without physical contact* or anything approaching it, a stage to which some practice with contact may be a necessary preliminary; in no other way can the hypothesis of " muscle-reading " be with certainty eliminated; while *en revanche*, the phenomena without contact, if once established, will afford solid ground for questioning the sufficiency of that hypothesis to account for all cases in which contact occurs.

Professor Balfour Stewart, LL.D., F.R.S., Professor of Physics at the Owens College, Manchester, made independent experiments with this family.   He says : We paid two visits to the house.   In the first instance, the thought-reader was outside a door.   The object or thing thought of was written on paper and silently handed round to the company in the room.   The thought-reader was then called in, and in the course, perhaps, of a minute the answer was given.   Definite objects in the room, for instance, were first thought of, and generally the answer was right.   Then cards were thought of, and in the majority of cases the answer was correct.   Then numbers were thought of, and the answers were generally right ; but, of course, there were some cases of error.   Then names of towns were thought of, and a good many of these were right.   Then fancy names were thought of.   When my colleague, Professor Hopkinson, had gone away, I was asked to think of certain fancy names, and mark them down and hand them round to the company.   I then thought of, and wrote on paper, " Blue-beard," " Tom Thumb," " Cinderella," and the answers were all correct.   I think it was the servant who answered " Cinderella."   There was some hesitation in getting her to pronounce the name, as she seemed to think she did not know it.

After the first visit, one of my colleagues at Owens College remarked that it would be more conclusive if the thought-reader, instead of turning her face to the company, turned her face to the wall; and that was accordingly done on the second occasion. The percentage of success was about as large as in the first instance. In one case, while the thought-reader *remained* behind the door, a card was chosen. I chose the " ace of hearts," and the paper on which it was written down was handed round to the company. The thought-reader in a few moments called out, " Ace of hearts ! "

The following is the detailed report of the experiments I have alluded to : —

On Saturday, Nov. 12, 1881, Professor Alfred Hopkinson and I went to the house of the Rev. A. M. Creery, at Buxton. There were present, besides Mr. Creery, Miss Mary Creery, also Alice, Emily, Maud, Kathleen, children; and the servant Jane.

After a few preliminary trials, the following guesses were made, the guesser going out of the room until some object was thought of by the company, when she came in and tried to guess what object was in the thoughts of all. No questions were asked nor observations made by the company : —

First. — DEFINITE OBJECTS THOUGHT OF.

1. *Pipe.* — Alice guessed paper, plate, then pipe.
2. *Fork.* — Maud guessed it at once.
3. *Cup.* — Emily guessed it at once.
4. *Corkscrew.* — Jane guessed it at once.
5. *Tongs.* — Miss Mary guessed fire-irons and then poker.

Second. — CARDS THOUGHT OF.

6. *Three of clubs.* — Jane guessed three of spades, then three of clubs.
7. *Queen of clubs.* — Miss Mary guessed three of diamonds.
8. *Four of clubs.* — Maud guessed five of clubs, then four of clubs.
9. *Ace of diamonds.* — Jane guessed ace of clubs, then ace of diamonds.

10. *King of spades.* — Jane guessed four of diamonds, then six of diamonds.

11. *King of hearts.* — Maud guessed knave of hearts, then king of hearts.

12. *Ace of spades.* — Maud guessed right at once.

13. *King of diamonds.* — Professor Stewart tried and guessed ten of diamonds.

14. *Three of diamonds.* — Miss Mary guessed right at once.

15. *Ace of hearts.* — Alice guessed right at once.

16. *King of clubs.* — Professor Hopkinson tried and guessed knave of spades, then four of hearts.

17. Mr. Creery and Professor Balfour Stewart tried, but could not guess.

Third. — Numbers Thought Of.

18. *Forty-eight .* — Jane guessed 34, 44, 84.

19. *Sixty-seven.* — Miss Mary guessed 66, then 67.

20. *Fifty-five.* — Maud guessed 54, 56, then 55.

21. *Eighty-one.* — Alice guessed 71, then 81.

22. *Thirty-one.* — Emily did not guess it.

23. *Eleven.* — Kathleen did not guess it.

Fourth. — Objects Thought Of.

Experiments 24, 25, 26, and 27, in which objects were thought of, were inconclusive, as the names of the things chosen might possibly have been surmised by the guesser.

Fifth. — Names of Towns Thought Of.

28. *Macclesfield.* — Jane did not guess rightly, then sat down, and shortly afterwards guessed rightly.

29. *York.* — Maud guessed Ashford, then York.

30. *Paris.* — Miss Mary did not guess rightly.

31. *Chester.* — Jane guessed Manchester, then Chester.

(N. B. — During this series also Mr. Creery was out of the room.)

Sixth. — FANCY NAMES.

32. *Peter Piper.* — Alice guessed at once.
33. *Bluebeard.* — Jane guessed at once.
34. *Tom Thumb.* — Jane guessed at once.
35. *Cinderella.* — Jane guessed at once.

I ought to state that the object thought of was marked on paper by one of the company, and handed round silently, so that all present might be aware of it.

I ought also to mention that the thought-reader was aware of the general character of the things thought of; for instance, that it was definite objects in the first place; cards in the second, and so on.

Professor Hopkinson agrees with the above memorandum, except that after No. 29, Derby was put down as the name of a town, and Maud guessed right the first time.

EXPERIMENTS AT BUXTON, FEB. 18, 1882. — Present : Mr. Creery and his five daughters; servant Jane; also Professors Hopkinson and Balfour Stewart.

GUESSER.	CARD SELECTED BY BALFOUR STEWART.	RESULT.
1. Jane	Six of hearts	Wrong.
2. Miss Alice . .	Knave of clubs . . .	"
3. Miss Maud . .	Seven of hearts . . .	Right 1st time.
4. " . .	Ten of spades . . .	" 1st time.
5. " . .	King of diamonds . .	" 2d time.
6. Miss Maud . .	Ace of hearts . . .	Wrong.
7. Miss Mary . .	Six of spades . . .	"
8. Jane	Ten of hearts . . .	Right 1st time.
9. "	Three of diamonds . .	Wrong.
10. "	Four of diamonds . .	"
11. "	Four of spades . . .	"
12. Miss Maud . .	Five of clubs	Right 3d time.
13. " . .	Six of hearts	" 2d time.
14. " . .	Queen of hearts . .	" 1st time.
15. Miss Alice . .	Two of diamonds . .	" 2d time.

	GUESSER.	CARD SELECTED BY BALFOUR STEWART.		RESULT.
16.	Miss Alice . .	Nine of diamonds . .	Right	3d time.
17.	" . .	Three of clubs . . .	"	3d time.
18.	" . .	Six of diamonds . .	"	3d time.
19.	" . .	King of spades . . .	"	2d time.
20.	" . .	Queen of spades . .	"	3d time.
21.	" . .	Knave of diamonds .	"	2d time.
22.	Miss Mary . .	Eight of clubs . . .	Wrong.	
23.	Jane	Five of diamonds . .	Right	1st time.
24.	"	Four of spades . . .	"	1st time.

(In the three next experiments the guesser remained outside the door.)

25.	"	Ace of hearts . . .	Right	1st time.
26.	"	Five of spades . . .	{ Wrong. Ace of spades guessed.	
27.	"	Five of diamonds . .	{ Wrong. Ace of diam'ds guessed.	

		NUMBER SELECTED BY BALFOUR STEWART.		
28.	Jane	22	Right	1st time.
29.	"	46	Wrong.	
30.	"	10	Right	1st time.
31.	"	12	Wrong.	
32.	Miss Maud . . .	44	Right	1st time.
33.	" . . .	37	"	1st time.
34.	" . . .	81	Wrong.	
35.	Miss Alice . . .	33	Right	1st time.
36.	" . . .	27	"	2d time.
37.	" . . .	55	Wrong.	
38.	Miss Mary . . .	66	"	
39.	Jane	28	"	
40.	"	43	"	
41.	"	22	"	

		OBJECT SELECTED BY BALFOUR STEWART.		
42.	Jane	A dish	Wrong.	
43.	Miss Maud . .	Cream jug	"	
44.	Miss Alice . .	Scissors	Right	1st time.

GUESSER.	OBJECT SELECTED BY BALFOUR STEWART.	RESULT.
45. Miss Alice . .	Prof. Hopkinson's hat,	Right 3d time.
46. " . .	Key	Wrong.
47. Miss Maud . .	Clothes brush . . .	Right 1st time.
48. " . .	Umbrella	Wrong.
49. Jane	Candlestick	"
50. "	Teapot	"
51. Miss Alice . .	Watch	"
52. " . .	Key	"
53. Miss Mary . .	Knife	Right 1st time.[1]
54. " . .	Pencil	" 1st time.
55. " . .	Toothpick	Doubtful.
56. " . .	A sovereign	Right 2d time.
57. Miss Maud . .	Purse	Wrong.

In all the above cases, except two or three, the guesser's back was turned to the company.

Mr. Turner, a medical man residing in Buxton, at the request of Mr. Creery, conducted some experiments, which he thus records : —

With a friend, who appends his signature to these notes, which are copied from those taken on the moment, I visited the Rev. A. M. Creery on Feb. 18, 1882, for the purpose of witnessing the power of thought-reading possessed by his children. In the absence of Mr. Creery, I made an attempt to test the children's power, and with the following results, roughly chronicled, I know, and imperfect as a searching test, but accurate as to the results obtained.

MISS ALICE CREERY.

Expt. 1. — What do I hold in my hand ? *Answer.* — Spectacles. (Describe them.) Eyeglasses. (I had Mr. Orme's eyeglasses concealed in my hand.)

Expt. 2. — What do I hold in my hand ? *Answer.* — Piece of paper. (No.) Knife. (Describe it.) It is white. (De-

[1] The knife was also correctly described by the guesser. It had not been out of Professor Hopkinson's pocket until after Miss Mary had left the room.

scribe further.)   It has a toothpick and button-hook.   (Correct;
it had other implements useful to a smoker.)

Expt. 3.—What do I hold in my hand?   *Answer.*—A ring.
(Describe it.)   Has a buckle on it.   (Correct.)

MISS MAUD CREERY.

Expt. 1.—What town have we thought of?   *Answer.* — Buxton.   (Correct.)

Expt. 2. — What town have we thought of?   *Answer.* —Derby.
(What part did you first think of?)   Railway station..   (So did
I.   Next.)   The market-place.   (So did I.)

Expt. 3. — What town have we thought of?   *Answer.* —Something commencing with L.   (Pause of a minute.)   Lincoln.
(Correct.)

Expt. 4. — What town have we thought of?   *Answer.* —
Stockport.   (Correct.)

Expt. 5. — What town have we thought of?   *Answer.* — Fair-
field.   (What part did you think of first?)   The road to it.   (So
did I.)   (What part next?)   The triangular green behind the
Bull's Head Inn.   (So did I.)

JANE DEAN, *the Maid Servant.*

Expt. 1. — What do I take hold of in my pocket?   *Answer.*—
Spectacle-case.   (Does it contain anything?)   It's empty.
(Correct.)

Expt. 2. — What have I placed under the piano?   *Answer.* —
A key.   (What is it the key of?)   A club.   (One and one-half
minute's pause.)   No.   The key of the Asylum.   (It was the
key of the Asylum grounds.   No one knew that I had a private
key; I am not officially connected with the Asylum.)

Expt. 3. — What have we agreed to think of?   *Answer.*—A
flower.   (What is the name of the flower?   Slight hesitation,
then answered.)   Lily of the valley.   (No.)   Immediately pointed
to some flowers in Mr. Orme's coat.   Snowdrop.   (Correct.)

Expt. 4. — What have I in my hand?   *Answer.*—A pin.
(What color.)   Black.   (What shape?)   Bending her index
finger and thumb into the shape of the letter C, she said, "That
shape."   Unknown to anyone I had bent it to that shape.)

Expt. 5. — What card have I selected?   *Answer.* — Seven of hearts. (No.) Eight of hearts. (Correct. Which way is the point of the heart directed?) Upwards. (Correct.)

Expt. 6. — What card have I selected? *Answer.* — Nine of spades. (Correct. Which way is the point of the spade directed?) Downwards. (Correct.)

No one knew of the previous card except Mr. Orme. No one knew of the second card except myself.

> FREDK. TURNER, M.R.C.S., Grafton House, Buxton.
> JOHN H. ORME, Solicitor, Buxton.

July 14, 1882.

The fourth head comprises cases where similar thoughts have simultaneously occurred, or impressions been made in minds far apart, without any known means of communication : —

Several cases of this kind have reached us, but they rest upon the testimony of others, and though we have no reason to doubt the accuracy of our informants, the evidence has necessarily a lower rank than the preceding. The following cases may be taken as a sample of other statements that have come to our knowledge. We are acquainted with, but not at liberty to publish, the names in the first case, which is related by the wife of General R ——.

"On Sept. 9, 1848, at the siege of Mooltan, Major-General R ——, C.B., then adjutant of his regiment, was most severely and dangerously wounded, and, supposing himself dying, asked one of the officers with him to take the ring off his finger and send it to his wife, who at the time was fully 150 miles distant, at Ferozepore.

"On the night of Sept. 9, 1848, I was lying on my bed, between sleeping and waking, when I distinctly saw my husband being carried off the field, seriously wounded, and heard his voice, saying, 'Take this ring off my finger, and send it to my wife.' All the next day I could not get the sight or the voice out of my mind. In due time I heard of General R —— having been severely wounded in the assault on Mooltan. He survived, however, and is still living. It was not for some time after the siege that I heard from Colonel L ——, the officer who helped to carry General R —— off the field, that the request as to the ring was actually made to him, just as I had heard it at Ferozepore at that very time. — M. A. R."

"LESLIE LODGE, EALING, W., Oct. 10, 1876.

"DEAR SIR, — The circumstance about which you inquire is as follows; I had left my house, ten miles from London, in the morning as usual, and in the course of the day was on my way to Victoria Street, Westminster, having reached Buckingham Palace, when in attempting to cross the road, recently made muddy and slippery by the water-cart, I fell, and was nearly run over by a carriage coming in an opposite direction. The fall and the fright shook me considerably, but beyond that I was uninjured. On reaching home I found my wife waiting anxiously, and this is what she related to me : She was occupied wiping a cup in the kitchen, which she suddenly dropped, exclaiming, 'My God! he's hurt.' Mrs. S., who was near her, heard the cry, and both agreed as to the details of time and so forth. I have often asked my wife why she cried out, but she is unable to explain the state of her feelings beyond saying, 'I don't know why; I felt some great danger was near you.' These are simple facts, but other things more puzzling have happened in connection with the singular intuitions of my wife.

"Yours truly,

"T. W. SMITH."

The next case is more remarkable ; our informant is a medical man, Mr. C. Ede, of Guildford, to whom the incident was related both by Lady G. and her sister.

"Lady G. and her sister had been spending the evening with their mother, who was in her usual health and spirits when they left her. In the middle of the night the sister awoke in a fright, and said to her husband, 'I must go to my mother at once; do order the carriage. I am sure she is taken ill.' The husband, after trying in vain to convince his wife that it was only a fancy, ordered the carriage. As she was approaching her mother's house, where two roads meet, she saw Lady G.'s carriage.

When they met, each asked the other why she was there. The same reply was made by both. 'I could not sleep, feeling sure my mother was ill, and so I came to see.' As they came in sight of the house, they saw their mother's confidential maid at the door, who told them, when they arrived, that their mother had been taken suddenly ill, and was dying, and had expressed an earnest wish to see her daughters."

The following interesting letter from Mr. Ede accompanied this narrative : —

"WONERSH LODGE, GUILDFORD, SURREY, Aug. 29, 1877.

"DEAR SIR, — The foregoing incident was told me as a simple narrative of what happened, both by Lady G. and her sister. The mother was a lady of strong will, and always had great influence over her daughters.

"I myself have been persuaded that impressions and thoughts might be transmitted by the action of a powerful will upon sensitive brains at a distance, by some experiments which I made in mesmerism, being at first a strong disbeliever in all these things, and only convinced when testing the assertions of others. There must, it would seem, be some previous relation between the two brains, as in states of anxiety for the absent, or powerful longing. May not a material vibration in a strong brain affect another by its vibration, as light at a distance acts upon the retina of the eye, or sound upon the ear ? We know that many sounds escape us if our attention be not directed to them, and, likewise, many objects may not be perceived. It is curious, in the case of Lady G. and her sister, that both impressions were made in the night, when the attention was not diverted by surrounding sights or sounds.

"This may have had some connection with the following incident which happened to myself lately. There is a house about half a mile from my own, inhabited by some ladies, friends of our family. They have a large alarm bell outside their house. One night I awoke suddenly and said to my wife, 'I am sure I hear Mrs. F.'s alarm bell ringing.' After listening for some time we heard nothing, and I went to sleep again. The next day Mrs. F. called upon my wife, and said to her, 'We were wishing for your husband last night, for we were alarmed by thieves. We were all up, and I was about to pull the alarm bell, hoping he would hear it, saying to my daughters, I am sure it will soon bring your husband, but we did not ring it.' My wife asked what time it was; Mrs. F. said it was about half past one. That was the time I awoke thinking I heard the bell.

"I could also give you many instances of the communication to another of a strong wish on my part, although unuttered, and unaccompanied by any gesture, or hint by look or action. I have often been amused at a concert, or other place of meeting, to single out some person who has their back to me, and will them to turn their head in a given direction towards me, and generally I succeed. It is common enough to have the same thoughts spoken by two people simultaneously, but, though the previous conversation might often suggest like ideas, I think it would not be difficult to sift out the cases of direct mental impressions from those of coincidence, suggestion, or sequence of thought arising from surrounding causes. When I have been strongly wishing to see a friend, it constantly happens that he appears. May not the many extraordinary cases of apparitions be but the mental pictures produced by other minds on a sensitive subject? There is a well-known case recorded in the Colonial papers which supports this view.

"Yours truly,

"CHARLES EDE."

Professor Barrett, in a separate paper submitted to this Society, says :—

Interesting and able articles on thought-reading have recently appeared in the "Spectator," together with several letters on the subject. The term *will-impression*, rather than thought-reading, is proposed by one correspondent in the "Spectator," and with much justice; the committee have accepted the ordinary phraseology simply because it has come into general use. Among the letters in the "Spectator" the following may be cited : —

"I had one day been spending the morning in shopping, and returned by train just in time to sit down with my children to our early family dinner. My youngest child — a sensitive, quick-witted, little maiden of two years and six weeks old — was one of the circle. Dinner had just commenced, when I suddenly recollected an incident in my morning's experience which I had intended to tell her, and I looked at the child with the full intention of saying, 'Mother saw a big, black dog in a shop, with curly hair,' catching her eyes in mine, as I paused an instant before speaking. Just then something called off my attention, *and the sentence was not uttered.* What was my amazement, about two minutes afterwards, to hear my little lady announce, 'Mother saw a big dog in a shop.' I gasped. 'Yes, I did!' I answered; 'but how did you know?' 'With funny hair?' she added, quite calmly, and ignoring my question. 'What color was it, Evelyn?' said one of her elder brothers; 'was it black?' She said, 'Yes.'

" Now, it was simply impossible that she could have received any hint of the incident verbally, I had had no friend with me when I had seen the dog. All the children had been at home, in our house in the country, four miles from the town; I had returned, as I said, just in time for the children's dinner, and I had not even remembered the circumstance until the moment when I fixed my eyes upon my little daughter's. We have had in our family circle numerous examples of spiritual or mental insight or foresight; but this, I think, is decidedly the most remarkable that has ever come under my notice.

" I am, Sir, etc.,
" CAROLINE BARBER.

"FERNDENE, ABBEYDALE, NEAR SHEFFIELD, June 22."

To the same journal the Suffragan Bishop of Bedford, Dr. Walsham How, contributes a remarkable case of perception at a distance, which came under the observation of his father. In this case the whole details of a distant *scene* were perceived in a dream, and with a minuteness that seemed to exclude any mere freak of the imagination on the part of the seer.

Several cases have come under my notice lately, of an accident or a wound in battle (*e. g.*, one in the Zulu war, and one in the present campaign in Egypt), occurring to some individual, and at the same instant a distant friend has received an intimation of the occurrence, very much as if a nervous thrill had passed through the intervening space, awakening a response in a sympathetic mind. These cases fall under the *fourth group of phenomena* mentioned in this report. I am indebted to Mrs. G. Bidder for the following additional evidence under this head : —
" A connection of mine was staying with a friend whose husband was engaged in making a line of railway in Spain. My friend was roused one night by her hostess, who was in a terrible fright, and said she was certain her husband was killed in a railway accident. She had been wakened with a start, and then had either seen the occurrence or been told in some way, but how, she could not remember. My friend reminded her that the railway he was engaged on did not open till the next day, so that the accident was unlikely. It turned out, however, that her husband had been doubtful of the safety of one part of the line, and had insisted on running an engine over it in the night, to try it for the next day's opening, and he had been killed."

In the memoir of the late Bishop Wilberforce, a similar transmission of an impression is recorded in the following words : —
" The Bishop was in his library at Cuddesdon, with three or four of his clergy writing with him at the same table. The Bishop suddenly raised his hand to his head, and exclaimed: 'I am certain that something has happened to one of my sons.' It afterwards transpired that just at that time his eldest son, who was at sea, had had his foot badly crushed by an accident on board his ship." The Bishop himself records this circumstance in a letter written at the time, and dated March 4, 1847. " It is curious," the Bishop writes, " that at the time of his accident, I was so possessed with the depressing consciousness of some evil having befallen my son Herbert, that at last, on the third day after, the 13th, I wrote down that I was quite unable to shake off the impression that something had happened to him, and noted this down for remembrance."

Dr. Wilton, of Sutton, Surrey, is my authority for the following case : —

"A patient of mine, Mr. J. T——, a solicitor, about sixty years of age, lived a short distance out of London, with his family, consisting of a wife and step-daughter, Miss W——. One December he was asked to go to Edinburgh, to arbitrate in some matter of business. Accordingly he left London, expecting to be away nearly a week.

"In the early morning of the third day after his departure, Mrs. T—— awoke, and was surprised to find her husband, as she thought, standing by her bedside. She exclaimed, 'How did you get in without my hearing you ? Wait while I light the candle.' She struck a match, and was very astonished at not seeing her husband in the room. While she was thinking over this singularly vivid delusion, her step-daughter, who occupied an adjoining room, knocked at the door, and, on being admitted, said, 'O mother, I have had a horrible dream about father, and cannot sleep; I am afraid something has happened to him.' In the morning they both told their stories to their maid, and subsequently to a gentleman who called while they were at breakfast. In the course of the forenoon a telegram arrived from Mr. T—— saying there had been an accident to the train in which he had been a passenger, that he was not hurt, and would be home in the course of the day.

"It appears that he had arranged his business much quicker than he had expected, and was able to leave Edinburgh by the night train ; a collision took place a few miles from London, owing to a thick fog, and about the time when the two ladies were disturbed by their dreams. There was no doubt whatever of the truth of this strange coincidence, the ladies having told their dreams long before the arrival of the telegram. I attended the family many years, and although Mr. T—— did not appear to have sustained injury at the time, he never recovered from the nervous shock."

The "Spectator" publishes the following : —

"My eldest brother went to New Zealand. One morning my sister Emily came down to breakfast, looking very white and

queer, and directly she entered the room, said, — 'Ben has met
with an accident.' Disregarding our incredulous amusement,
she declared she had seen him with his arm bandaged up, lying
in a room where there were other beds. We were longer than
usual in hearing from my brother; he explained the delay,
saying his arm had been broken, and that he had been for some
time in the hospital. Comparing dates, we found he was in-
jured the day my sister had her vision. — I am, Sir,

"ANTHONY ASHLEY."

"3 Buxton Villas, Stratford, August 7."

Other cases are doubtless known to many who read this, for a
multitude of similar stories are in existence. Hitherto, as these
facts arose, the general explanation has been coincidence. It
has been said, "How many thousands of accidents occur, and
no knowledge of them has been conveyed to others, except
through the ordinary means; but when, by a fortuitous circumstance or a natural foreboding, some friend fancies an accident
has occurred, and it turns out more or less as imagined, then
such coincidences are talked about as if they were representative, or indicative of a law, whereas they are really nothing
more than chance shots." This would be a legitimate argument
if the cases were excessively rare, and so far as our knowledge of
the facts extends at present, we are not in a position to do more
than assert that enough well-authenticated cases are on record
to render explanation by coincidence difficult to entertain with
any degree of confidence. When to this is added the facts
detailed in our report — from which I venture to think the only
fair conclusion is that some mode of supersensuous perception
not improbably exists — then it seems to me unphilosophical to
reject, as unworthy of serious examination, all stories such as
those just narrated. On the other hand — reiterating what has
been emphatically stated already — wide generalizations are
altogether premature. Our object here, as elsewhere, is simply
to collect, collate, and weigh the facts, using, if need be, as a
working hypothesis, the conclusions drawn from our Buxton
experiments.

Nor must we forget that other workers have been in this or an adjoining field. A list of well-known names might easily be compiled who have testified from critical observation that during the mesmeric sleep the mind of the mesmeriser can influence that of the subject, independently of the ordinary channels of sensation.

The late Dr. Bush, a distinguished scholar, and Professor in the University of New York, writes : —" I know that the conceptions of my own mind have been reproduced in another mind without any outward signs, and I know that I have not been deceived as to the facts averred."

Dr. Mayo, F.R.S., who was Professor of Physiology and Anatomy in King's College, London, and the author of an important treatise on " The Nervous System and its Functions," gives similar testimony. In connection with this subject, he remarks : — " A number of incidents are frequently turning up, for the most part on trivial occasions, which we put aside for fear of being thought superstitious, because as yet a natural solution is not at hand for them. Sympathy in general, the spread of panic fears, the simultaneous occurrence of the same thoughts to two persons, the intuitive knowledge of mankind possessed by some, the magnetic fascination of others, may eventually be found to have to do with a special and unsuspected cause."

The principle underlying these occurrenees Dr. Mayo believes to be the same that is found in a more striking form in mesmeric phenomena. Of the singular relationship that exists between the minds of the mesmeriser and his subject, producing an apparent community of thought and sensation, Dr. Mayo gives experimental evidence precisely similar to what has come under my own observation, and in conclusion he states : — " I hold that the mind of a living person in its most normal state is always, to a certain extent, acting exoneurally, or beyond the limits of the bodily person." He remarks that, " It will be said that the cases in which I suppose this power manifested are of too trivial a nature to justify so novel an hypothesis. My answer is, the cases are few and trivial only because the subject has not been attended to. For how many centuries were the laws of electricity pre-indicated by the single fact that a piece of amber, when rubbed, would attract light bodies. Again, the school of physiological materialists will of course be opposed to it. They hold that the mind is but a function or product of the brain."[1]

As we have stated in the Report, we have been anxious to accumulate and sift experimental evidence as to the facts before us, rather than to indulge in theories as to the cause of the phenomena. We may, however, conceive of nervous energy acting by induction across space as well as by conduction along the nerve fibres. In fact the numerous analogies between electricity and nervous stimuli would lead to some such inference as the above. Or the brain might be regarded as the seat of radiant energy like a glowing or a sounding body. In this case, the reception of the energy would depend upon a possibility of synchronous vibration in the absorbing body ; which, moreover, may be constituted like a sensitive flame, in a state of unstable equilibrium, so that a distant mental disturbance might suddenly and profoundly agitate particular minds whilst others might remain quiescent. Further, we may conceive that, just as a vibrating tuning-fork or string spends its energy most swiftly when it is exciting another similar fork or string in unison with itself, so the activity of the brain may be more speedily exhausted by the presence of other brains capable of sympathetic vibration with itself.

But speculations such as these are merely of use in suggesting lines of experiment. For my own part, I have little doubt that a wider and more exact knowledge of psychological phenomena will show the insufficiency of any physical analogy or materialistic explanation, and thus should tend to accelerate the passage of the existing wave of materialism, the crest of which, there seems reason to believe, has already gone over us.

The following extract from a letter in the " Sussex Daily News " is of some interest in connection with the mode of experiment pursued by Mr. Bishop. The subject of thought-reading having

---

[1] " Truths contained in Popular Superstitions," p. 68 et seq.

been discussed, "It was proposed that we should attempt the experiment. Accordingly I was blindfolded and left the room. Whilst I was absent, a reel of black cotton was secreted in a flower-pot near the window. On pressing the hand of the gentleman who had secreted it against my forehead, and requesting him to think of the object he had hidden, I saw plainly with my blindfolded eyes, as though in a dream, the figure of a reel of black cotton floating before me. I then told him to think of where he had hidden it, and I saw and led him to a bureau at the opposite end of the room to the window. This he said was wrong, but on inquiry I found that he had originally intended to have placed it there, but had altered his mind. We then tried the question of localizing a pain. Being blindfolded, and holding my friend's left hand against my forehead, I told him to imagine a pain. Almost immediately I felt a peculiar, indescribable sensation on the right side of my face, and told him that he was thinking of a pain there. He was, in fact, imagining a violent attack of neuralgia in the right upper jaw. Other experiments were tried, and have been tried since, some successful, some unsuccessful, but I have seen quite enough to convince me that there is truth in it. I don't pretend to offer a reason, but I would say to those who disbelieve it, 'Try for yourselves.' All do not possess the power. I was the only one of a party of six or seven who was thus affected, but, doubtless, there are very many who could perform precisely the same experiments, and by continued inquiry it may be that the mystery will be solved. — I am yours, &c.,

"HENRY EDMONDS, B. Sc. (London).
" Brighton School of Science and Art."

The following extract from a letter published in "Light" shows that a Mr. Smith, of Brighton, has powers analogous to those claimed by Mr. Bishop : — "The way Mr. Smith conducts his experiment is this : He places himself *en rapport* with myself by taking my hands ; and a strong concentration of will and mental vision on my part has enabled him to read my thoughts with an accuracy that approaches the miraculous. Not only can he, with slight hesitation, read numbers, words, and even whole sentences which I alone have seen, but the sympathy between us has been developed to such a degree that he rarely fails to experience the taste of any liquid or solid I choose to imagine. He has named, described, or discovered small articles he has never seen when they have been concealed by me in the most unusual places, and on two occasions he has successfully described portions of a scene which I either imagined or actually saw.

"DOUGLAS BLACKBURN, Editor of 'Brightonian.'

"24 Duke Street, Brighton."

Mr. Bishop has lately been good enough to give me an opportunity of trying his powers. In the first instance, by means of a confederate, he showed the wonderful perfection to which he has carried fictitious thought-reading, indicating objects, names, or figures by means of a pre-arranged code. Thus his confederate, who was seated back to us and blindfolded in another part of the room, told us, — in answer to a succession of seemingly casual questions on the part of Mr. Bishop — the whole particulars of a Bank of England cheque which a friend of mine happened to have in his pocket, the nature, number, and date of the cheque, the person in whose favor it was drawn, the person who drew the cheque, and the bankers in whose favor it was crossed; Mr. Bishop, of course, looking at the cheque from time to time. Mr. Bishop then showed what he believes to be the genuine power of thought-reading that he possesses. Some striking things were done; for example, he wrote with his finger on the door certain figures corresponding to those that I had put on paper and was thinking of, but had shown to no one else, his hand pressing mine tightly against his forehead. He also twice discovered the exact locality of a pain that I fixed upon, in one case with extreme accuracy, but he did not succeed so well with a friend; in this case also he pressed the hand of the subject against his own forehead. He next tried some experiments without contact, his hand being held very near mine; in this way he moved backwards and forwards across the room in the precise direction that I had previously, in his absence, written down; other experiments without contact were not quite so successful. It is, however, very difficult to arrive at any satisfactory conclusions from these experiments, owing to the extraordinary pantomime and wriggling excited action which Mr. Bishop invariably employs, so utterly different from the silent, passive condition to which we have been accustomed in the experiments recorded in our report.

In closing its first report the Committee on Thought-Transference says : —

We cannot pretend that this inquiry is as yet more than in its infancy, and we would deprecate the premature formation of theories on the subject. The phenomena here described are so unlike any which have been brought within the sphere of recognized science, as to subject the mind to two opposite dangers. Wild hypotheses as to how they happen are confronted with equally wild assertions that they cannot happen at all. Of the two, the assumption of *à priori* impossibility is, perhaps, in the present state of our knowledge of Nature, the most to be deprecated; though it cannot be considered in any way surprising.

At the same. time it may. serve to disarm purely *à priori* criticism if we point out that the word " thought-reading " is merely used as a popular and provisional description, and is in no way intended to exclude an explanation resting on a physical basis. It is quite open to surmise some sort of analogy to the familiar phenomena of the transmission and reception of vibratory energy. A swinging pendulum suspended from a solid support will throw into synchronous vibration another pendulum attached to the same support, if the period of oscillation of the two be the same; the medium of transmission here being the solid material of the support. One tuning-fork or string in unison with another will communicate its impulses through the medium of the air. Glowing particles of a gas, acting through the medium of the luminiferous ether, can throw into sympathetic vibration cool molecules of the same substance at a distance. A permanent magnet brought into a room will throw any surrounding iron into a condition similar to its own; and here the medium of communication is unknown, though the fact is undisputed. Similarly, we may conceive, if we please, with many modern philosophers, that for every thought there is a corresponding motion of the particles of the brain, and that this vibration of molecules of brain-stuff may be communicated to an intervening medium, and so pass under certain circumstances from one brain to another, with a corresponding simultaneity of impressions. No more than in the case of the magnetic phenomena is any investigator bound to determine the *medium* before inquiring into the *fact* of transit. On the other hand, the possibility must not be overlooked that further advances along the lines of research here indicated may, and we believe will, necessitate a modification of that general view of the relation of mind to matter to which modern science has long been gravitating.

III.

THE second report of the Committee on Thought-Transference was submitted to the Society Dec. 9, 1882. It was as follows:—

The first Report of the Committee on Thought-reading, presented to the Society on July 17, 1882, established, as we venture to affirm, the following conclusions:—

(1). That much of what is popularly known as "Thought-reading" is in reality due to the interpretation by the so-called "Reader" of signs, consciously or unconsciously imparted by the touches, looks, or gestures of those present; and that this is to be taken as the *primâ facie* explanation, whenever the thing thought of is not some visible or audible object, but some action or movement to be performed.

(2). That there does exist a group of phenomena to which the word "thought-reading," or, as we prefer to call it, *thought-transference*, may be fairly applied; and which consist in the mental perception, by certain individuals at certain times, of a word or other object kept vividly before the mind of another person or persons, without any transmission of impression through the recognized channels of sense.

We have been fortunate enough to obtain a much larger amount of adhesion to this view than its startling character had permitted us to expect. Some valuable coadjutors have shown their approval by joining our body; and the wide notice which has been taken of the research, in the press and in society, has started, we trust, many sets of experiments, from which useful results may be fairly anticipated. Criticism has, of course, been by no means entirely favorable, and we had had some idea of prefacing our description of further experiments by a detailed reply to some of the objections which have been taken to our former report. But an attentive study of those objections has failed to supply us with much controversial matter worthy of occupying the time of the present meeting. They may, we think, be completely answered from the pages of the Report itself.   One lesson, indeed, our critics have taught us,— the importance of the directest statements, and the largest letters, in a paper containing complex or novel matter, which is to meet the eye of the ordinary reviewer.   For most of the criticisms on our first Report were founded on the assumption that it does *not* contain what in fact it *does* contain, — if only the reader will take the trouble to read it.   To take the main point, we based our conviction of the reality of the phenomena on experiments made *when none of the Creery family were cognizant of the object selected.* A feeling of courtesy (not, we trust, necessarily unscientific) prevented us from saying, in so many words, " It will thus be seen that our results hold good, however much the Creery family may have been in league to cheat us."

We fully agree with our critics that both conscious and unconscious deception must be most carefully guarded against in all these cases.   We shall continue to take all the precautions which experience suggests, and clearly to indicate in our Reports that we have taken them.   But we must beg our future reviewers to read those reports with sufficient care to absolve us from saying in plain words, at every turn, " This we did to prevent Mr. A. from slyly glancing at the card ; " " This precaution was taken for fear Miss B. should be telling a lie."   It is part of the wisdom of the serpent not to discuss too obtrusively the harmlessness of the dove.

We could easily reply *seriatim* to all the objections that have been brought; as, for instance, that we have not stated that silence was preserved during the experiments, whereas we *have* stated it over and over again ; or that the child might have known which card we were likely to choose, whereas we have stated that the cards were drawn at random from a full pack. Does the hypothesis, further, include the likelihood of the child's guessing that our minds would be irresistibly directed to the names Arthur Higgins and Esther Ogle, names which we trust our free-will enough to believe that we invented in the act of writing them down ?   Such detailed refutation, however obvious, might possibly be worth working through, did the whole case for thought-reading depend on this *one* series of experiments. As the case stands, however, we think we may fairly pass on, without more ado, to fresh matter.

The chief part of the first Report dealt with a series of experiments on thought-reading made at Buxton, with the young daughters of the Rev. A. M. Creery. The committee felt it desirable that the experiments with this family should be repeated elsewhere, and accordingly Mr. Myers invited the committee to meet the Misses Creery at his house, Leckhampton, Cambridge, during the summer vacation. In addition to Mr. Myers, Mr. Gurney, and Mr. Barrett, Mrs. Myers and Miss M. Mason were also present.

The experiments began on July 31, 1882, and were continued day by day for ten days. The experiments were made with the three Misses Creery, — Mary, age 17, Alice, age 15, Maud, 13, — and were varied in many ways. Sometimes (though in a decided minority of cases) the two children who were not guessing knew what we had selected. The percentage of success in these cases was not appreciably above the average percentage of the whole series. Sometimes the guesser was outside a thick closed door, sometimes secluded by a thick curtain, in full observation of one of the committee. On several occasions the children were tested, one by one, alone. Professor Barrett's results under these conditions, and Miss Mason's under the same conditions, and with the child outside the door, were decidedly striking.

The fluctuations in success were very remarkable. Thus, on one day, August 1, when the guesser was outside the closed door, twenty-seven trials with cards gave not a single correct result; merely seven partial successes, as eight of diamonds for seven of diamonds. Whereas on August 3, apparently under precisely similar conditions, the guesser being outside the closed door, and no sound of any kind permitted within the room where we, who knew the card, sat, ten trials gave two completely right and two almost right; and on August 4, twenty-five trials, under exactly the same conditions, gave two completely right and two partially right.

Here are the details of the trials on August 3.

Evening of August 3, 1882.

Miss Mary Creery outside the closed and locked door, and a yard or two from it, in the company of one of the committee, who observed her attentively. A card chosen by one of the committee cutting a pack; the fact of the card being selected indicated to the guesser by a single tap on the door. The selected card placed in view of all the sitters, who kept their minds intently fixed on the name of the card. After the guesser had named a card loudly enough to be heard through the door, the words "No" or "Right" said by one of us; otherwise complete silence preserved.

The cards chosen by us are printed in italics, the guesses in Roman type. Two guesses only allowed.

1. *Three of hearts.* — Ten of spades (No). King of clubs (No).

2. *Seven of clubs.* — Nine of diamonds (No). Seven of hearts (No).

3. *Ten of diamonds.* — Queen of spades (No). Ten of diamonds (Right).

4. *Eight of spades.* — King of clubs (No). Ten of spades (No).

5. *Nine of hearts.* — Nine of clubs (No). Ace of hearts (No).

6. *Three of diamonds.* — Six of diamonds (No). Ten of diamonds (No).

7. *Knave of spades.* — King of spades (No). Queen of clubs (No).

8. *Six of spades.* — Six of spades (Right).

9. *Queen of clubs.* — Queen of diamonds (No). Ten of clubs (No).

10. *Two of clubs.* — Ten of diamonds (No). Ace of diamonds (No).

It may be remarked that, in addition to the two completely right answers in this series, there were several close approximations; and though the success was very imperfect, we give the result in detail, in order that those who feel disposed may,

experimentally, compare them with any series determined by
chance alone.

Anxiety to secure success on the part of the subject of experiment is nearly always fatal and always prejudicial; hence the
little trepidation that exists when set trials are made, or trials
before strangers, tells most unfavorably. We found that casual
experiments, when the subject was under no mental restraint,
gave very satisfactory results, albeit on such occasions our precautions to avoid erroneous convictions were in no way relaxed.

On the morning of August 4 such a casual trial was made,
Mrs. Myers and Professor Barrett only knowing the card selected.
Eight experiments were made ; of these, three cards were guessed
completely right — two of them at the first attempt and the third
at the second attempt. In this last case the first guess was the
nine of clubs, the second the nine of spades, that being the card
chosen. In addition to these the suit was given rightly three out
of the remaining five times, the pips or court card twice out of
the five. It is instructive to note that immediately after this
experiment the two younger sisters of the guesser were called
in and allowed to know the card chosen by Mrs. Myers and
Professor Barrett. The results, compared with the preceding,
were as follows : —

Without the sisters knowing. — Eight trials. Completely right
three times, two of them the first try.

With the sisters knowing. — Seven trials. Completely right
three times, two of them on the first trial; and to make the
coincidences more curious, the partial successes were identical
in number with the previous trial.

Other casual trials were made by single members of the committee, he alone knowing the word or card selected.

Thus, on August 5, Professor Barrett tried with Miss Creery
numbers of two figures; two attempts were generally allowed to
each. The following results were obtained. The number
chosen is in italics : —

ANSWER.	ANSWER.
18. 16 and then 18 were said.	*48.* 48 said at once.
29. 26 " 29 "	*31.* 71 and then 61.

ANSWER.				ANSWER.			
52. 35 and then 25 were said.				*21*. 22 said (one trial only given).			
33. 53	"	58	"	*36*. 16	"	"	
76. 17	"	36	"	*28*. 28	"	"	
				92. 10	"	"	

Here, out of 11 experiments, four were guessed rightly (2 at the
first attempt), and 4 bore some resemblance to the figure chosen,
as 25 the inversion of 52, the number chosen. This inversion
of figures not infrequently occurred, together with what seemed
like piecemeal guessing of the figures, which were, of course,
counted as failures, such as 17 and 36 for 76. These guesses
may be nothing more than pure coincidence, but taken in conjunction with our similar experience with cards, they would
seem to indicate that often mental glimpses of the thing selected
are obtained, more or less faint and fugitive, and sometimes
perverted, as if the figures had been seen from their reflection
in a mirror.

A remarkable instance of this partial perception of the thing
selected occurred on August 2. On this occasion all the Committee were present; two of the sisters of the guesser were also
in the room, and knew the card selected; they were, however,
so placed that (though they were completely in our view) only
the tops of their heads were visible to the guesser, and they
remained quite motionless and silent throughout the experiments. Out of 32 experiments with cards, 5 were guessed completely right at the first attempt, and, in addition, 20 were
partially right. *Fourteen times running* the suit was named
correctly on the first trial, and reiterated on the second; not
only was no indication whatever given to show that the suit was
rightly named, but our impassive countenances and the solitary
word "No" failed to displace from the percipient's mind the
correct impression of the suit. The chances against success in
naming the suit rightly in any one case are, of course, 3 to 1, but
the chances against being right fourteen times *consecutively* are
4,782,969 to 1. That is to say, if the words "clubs," "diamonds," "hearts," and "spades" were written on slips of card
and shaken up in a bag, we might very likely have to try four

or five million times before pulling out, fourteen times in succession, the particular word fixed upon.

To vary the wearisome monotony of our experiments, a number of trials were made at Cambridge in piecing together the letters of certain difficult words fixed upon by us. The letters forming the word, — which was always some out-of-the way Latin or botanical term unlikely to be divined by mere guesswork, — were selected by us from a box of letters; the confused heap was then taken to one of the Misses Creery, who was seated in an adjoining room. Some of these trials were very successful, but we abandoned this method of experiment as open to the possible objection that even children might gain some hint of the sequence of letters from an instinct of the probabilities of language. We give, however, a couple of instances out of some twenty similar trials. Here none but one or two of ourselves knew the word selected; the letters were chosen by us and then mixed up; the guesser, seated with her back to us, picked out the letters as we silently and successively thought of them. The figures under the letters indicate the number of trials before success was obtained; thus, 1 means right on the first trial, 2 right on the second, and so on. No word was spoken except "No" and "Yes."

H e d y p n o i s   P h y s a l o i d e s

1 1 1 2 1 1 1 1   1 2 4 1 1 1 1 4 1 1 1

Not reckoning these experiments with letters, our experiments during the meeting of the full committee at Cambridge may be summed up as follows : —

With a full pack of playing cards, 248 trials were made with one or more of the committee. Of these, 22 were guessed completely right on the first trial, and 18 on the second trial, or a total of 40 quite right out of 248; or 1 right in not quite 7 experiments. In addition, there were 69 cases in which the card was guessed in part correctly. *Omitting the second correct guess, the results with playing cards show one quite right in 11 experiments; if pure guesswork were the explanation, there would have been about one right in 52 experiments.*

With the exception of the 32 experiments described above, and which we deemed so unexceptionable that they were included, all these experiments were made when the Misses Creery were excluded from a knowledge of the card we had selected.

In like manner, while we alone knew the thing selected, 64 trials were made with *figures* ranging between 10 and 99. Of these, 5 were correctly named at the first trial, and 6 at the second — a total of 11 right out of 64, or about 1 in 6; and, in addition, 18 trials were nearly right. *Omitting the second correct guess, the results with figures show one right in not quite 13 experiments; pure guesswork would have given about one right in 90 experiments.*

Two of the Misses Creery having lately been on a visit to Dublin, one of our number, Professor Barrett, took the opportunity of continuing the trials, and obtained some interesting results. Here also a series of trials were made with the young percipient secluded behind an opaque curtain; her sister was allowed to know the card, but no audible signal could pass without its instant detection, and visual signs were rendered impossible.[1] In this way 14 trials, made on Nov. 27, with a full pack of playing cards, gave 4 completely right on the first try, and 2 on the second try; and, in addition, on an analysis of the results, the name of the suit was found to have been correctly given five times running, and reiterated on the second trial. Some experiments made under exactly similar conditions, a day or two later, gave 2 successes on the first trial out of a total of 8, and, except in the last trial, the suit was named correctly each time; here only one answer in each case was allowed. These, it is true, are specimens of results where the amount of success was above the average; which may, perhaps, partly be accounted for by the sister's assistance in the mental picturing of the card, or

---

[1] Although our previous experience had not much favored the suggestion, it was thought desirable further to test whether some *rapport* or sympathetic relation between the sisters might conduce to the desired result. This explains my allowing the other sister to be present and see the card in some of these experiments. — W. F. B.

by the percipient's having had a long respite from the irksome effort of concentration; but doubtless the chief element of success in this case was freedom from anxiety, as the percipient believed they were mere casual experiments, and could not see that the results were being formally taken down.

Altogether, in Professor Barrett's house, 109 trials were made with playing cards: of these, 19 were right on the first trial, and 7 on the second, and, in addition, 2 others were rightly corrected on a third attempt, though to grant this was against our usual practice. Altogether, this makes 28 completely right out of 109, and 26 other trials were nearly right. *But confining ourselves to the first guess, the results showed 1 right in not quite 6 trials; pure guesswork would give 1 right in 52 trials.* In the large majority of these trials the second sister did *not* know the card selected.

One hundred and forty-three experiments were also made with words and figures, Professor Barrett *only* knowing the thing he had selected. The chance was here more limited, being on an average about 1 in 16. Of these 143 experiments, 53 were quite successful on the first and 23 on the second trial. *Excluding the second trial, the successful results were rather more than 1 in 3; pure chance would have given 1 in 16.* For the purpose of comparison, 27 experiments were made, in which the other sister was allowed to be present and to know the figure, this being selected as before out of a set of 16. Out of the 27 experiments, 8 were successful on the first trial, and 1 on the second; omitting this, we have rather less than 1 in 3 right, showing that the presence and assistance of the sister here made no appreciable difference in the results.

A consecutive series of 50 experiments were made at one sitting to test the effect of fatigue. Besides Professor Barrett and Miss Alice Creery, who was seated with her back to the former, *no one else was present in the room.* The words "hearts," "clubs," "spades," and "diamonds" were written down by Mr. Barrett, and one of these words mentally selected by him.[1] Out of the 50

---

[1] The percipient, it should be remarked, knew that these four words were

trials, the word selected was named rightly 25 times on the first trial; and a second trial being allowed (though of no value as a test), the right answer was then given 10 times, making a total of 35 out of 50. The series occupied about 20 minutes, and the guessing was slower in the latter half of the time.

During the first 10 minutes.

30 experiments were made.

Of these 18 were right on the first trial.

    8 "   " second trial.

 or 4 wholly wrong.

During the second 10 minutes.

20 experiments were made.

Of these, 7 were right on the first trial.

    2 "   " second trial.

 or 11 wholly wrong.

So that about 1 in 7 trials was wholly wrong in the first half of the time, and about 1 in 2 was wrong in the second half.

It was also noticed incidentally that the longer word, "diamonds," was guessed with more difficulty than the remaining monosyllables, thus —

"Diamonds" was wholly wrong 6 times out of 12.

"Spades"   " " 2 " 11.

"Hearts"   " " 3 " 13.

"Clubs"   " " 4 " 14.

Indications were given in other trials, made with a selection of monosyllables phonetically unlike, that certain sounds were guessed more easily than others; thus, the word *cups* was more frequently wrong than *tongs* or *hats*. But a much larger range of experiments is needed before any generalization in this direction can be attempted. It will probably be remarked that the

selected, and she was to guess one of them. We hope the reader will credit us with being fully alive to the fact of the necessity of avoiding any movement which might serve as a hint to the guesser.

average of success in the above experiments, though far above what chance alone could have supplied, falls considerably below the level attained in the trials with the same children which were described in our previous report; and (as will have been seen) this decline in power equally showed itself whether the remaining members of the Creery family were or were not cognizant of the object to be guessed. The fact seems to be (and the children themselves are regretfully conscious of it) that the capacity is gradually leaving them, — a fresh illustration of the fleeting character which seems to attach to this and other forms of abnormal sensitiveness. *En revanche*, we find the capacity present, to a degree admitting of valuable experiment, in a far larger number of persons than we had at first supposed. To those who desire to extend knowledge in this direction, the following queries suggest lines of useful inquiry : —

1. A natural impressibility being assumed, what are the further conditions which determine or modify success.

2. Is the transferred impression phonetic, or visual, or indeterminate ?

3. How far do impressions of drawings or geometrical figures, inexpressible in descriptive words, admit of being transferred ?

4. Are there any peculiar features in this latter form of transference, such as the inversion or perversion of the object, etc. ?

To the third query we have unexpectedly received from some recent experiments a most definite and satisfactory answer. With a description of these experiments we must conclude the present report.

Mr. Blackburn, of Brighton, an associate of our Society, and who is a very painstaking and accurate observer, had obtained remarkable results in thought-reading, or will-impression, with a Mr. G. A. Smith, a young mesmerist living at Brighton.

We entered into correspondence with Mr. Blackburn, who thereupon took the trouble to send us a paper recording in detail his experiments with Mr. Smith. These statements appeared to be so carefully made that two of our number, Mr.

Myers and Mr. Gurney (Mr. Barrett being unable to go at the time), arranged to pay a visit to Brighton personally to investigate the joint experiments of Mr. Blackburn and Mr. Smith. These gentlemen most obligingly placed themselves at our service, and a series of trials were made in our own lodgings at Brighton. The results of these trials give us the most important and valuable insight into the manner of the mental transfer of a picture which we have yet obtained.

Mr. Blackburn has frequently practised thought-reading with Mr. Smith; but at the time when our first experiments were made, he had been accustomed to hold Mr. Smith's hand, or touch his forehead, with a view to communicating the impression. No unconscious pressure, however, could have communicated to the subject the definite words and pictures enumerated below. Though some of the early experiments are not striking, we prefer to give the whole series, that a due estimate may be formed of the chances against mere coincidence as an explanation.

EXPERIMENTS MADE AT OUR OWN ROOMS, BRIGHTON, DEC. 3, 1882. Present: Mr. Edmund Gurney, Mr. F. W. H. Myers, Mr. Douglas Blackburn, hereafter called B., and Mr. G. A. Smith, hereafter called S.

S. was blindfolded at his own wish, to aid in concentration, and during the experiment sat with his back turned to the experimenters.

B. holds S.'s hand, and asks him to name a color, written down by one of us and shown to B. It is needless to say the strictest silence was preserved during each experiment.[1]

	COLOR SELECTED.	ANSWER.
Expt. 1.	Gold	Gilt, color of picture frame.
" 2.	Light wood	Dark brown, slaty.
" 3.	Crimson	Fiery-looking, red.
" 4.	Black	Dark, black.

[1] Nothing was said when S. named the color, and where more than one color is mentioned he gave the colors successively without fresh question.

	COLOR SELECTED.	ANSWER.
Expt. 5.	Oxford blue	Yellow, gray, blue.
" 6.	White	Green, white.
" 7.	Orange	Reddish brown.
" 8.	Black	I am tired, and see nothing.

After a rest, *numbers* were then tried in the same way.

	NUMBER SELECTED.	ANSWER.
Expt. 9	35	34
" 10	48	58
" 11	7	7

Several trials of colors and numbers were now made with S. and B. in separate rooms, which failed. *Names* were next tried, written down and shown to B., who then took S.'s hand as before. There was, as usual, no sound nor movement of the lips on the part of any one.

	NAME CHOSEN.	ANSWER.
Expt. 12.	Barnard . . .	Harland, Barnard.
" 13.	Bellairs . . .	Humphreys, Ben Nevis, Benaris.
" 14.	Johnson . . .	Jobson, Johnson.
" 15.	Regent Street .	Rembrandt Steeth, Regent Street.

Two names were then tried without any contact, as follows: —

	NAME CHOSEN.	ANSWER.
Expt. 16.	Hobhouse	Hunter.
" 17.	Black	Drake, Blake.

Contact between S. and B. was now resumed by our express desire, as the increased effort of concentration, needed when there was no contact, brought on neuralgia in B.

	NAME CHOSEN.	ANSWER.
Expt. 18.	Queen Anne	Queechy, Queen.
" 19.	Wissenschaft	Wissie, Wissenaft.

As B. was ignorant of German, he mentally represented the word "Wissenschaft" in English fashion.

Pains were then experimented on. One of us held a sofa cushion close before S.'s face, so that vision of anything on the other side of it was absolutely impossible (he was also blindfolded); and the other pinched or otherwise hurt B., who sat opposite S., holding his outstretched hand. S. in each case localized the pain in his own person, after it had been kept up pretty severely upon B.'s person for a time varying from one to two minutes.

	PART RENDERED PAINFUL.	ANSWER (by pointing).
Expt. 20.	Left upper arm . . .	Left upper arm.
" 21.	Lobe of right ear . . .	Lobe of right ear.
" 22.	Hair on top of head . .	Hair on top of head.
" 23.	Left knee	Left knee.

These experiments were very striking in the accuracy of the indications given by S. This form of transmission of sensations might with advantage be more widely attempted.

We next drew a series of diagrams of a simple geometrical kind, which were placed behind S., so that B. could see them. S. described them in each case correctly, except that he generally reversed them, seeing the upper side of the diagram downward, the right-hand side to the left, etc.

Next day (December 4) we varied this experiment, thus : —

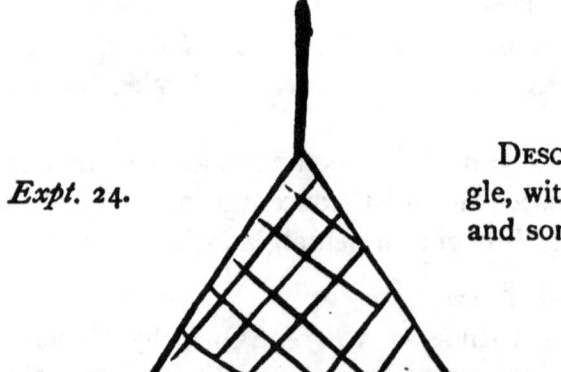

Expt. 24.

DESCRIPTION. — A triangle, with apex *downwards;* and some loose lines.

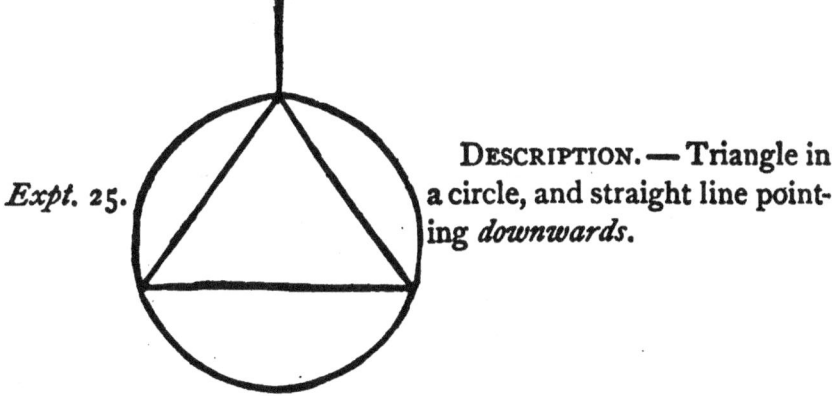

Expt. 25.

DESCRIPTION. — Triangle in a circle, and straight line pointing *downwards.*

Expt. 26. — A large arrow was drawn, and variously moved about, in order to discover whether the reversal of the image was maintained. In every case it was described as pointing to *right* when it pointed to *left*, *downwards* when it pointed *upwards*, and so on.

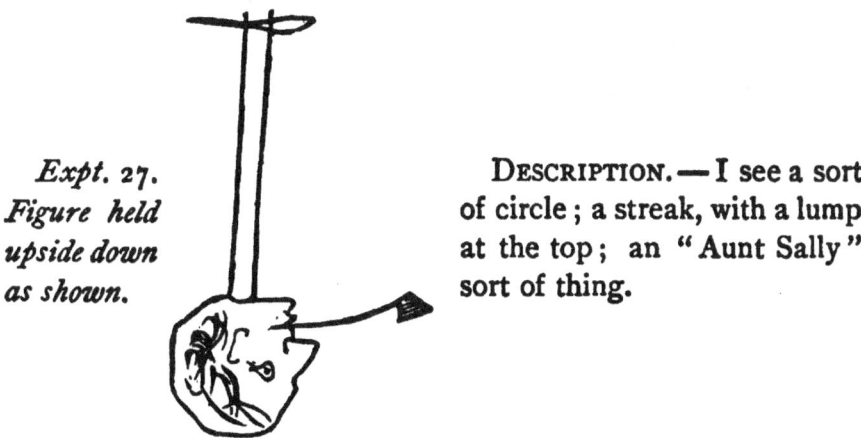

Expt. 27.
Figure held upside down as shown.

DESCRIPTION. — I see a sort of circle; a streak, with a lump at the top; an "Aunt Sally" sort of thing.

One of us, completely out of sight of S., drew some figure at random, the figure being of such a character that its shape could not be easily conveyed in words; this was done in order to meet the assumption that some code — such as the Morse alphabet — was used by S. and B. The figure drawn by us was then shown to B. for a few moments, — S. being seated all the time with his back to us and blindfolded, in a distant part of the same room, and subsequently in an adjoining room.

B. looked at the figure drawn; then held S.'s hand for a while; then released it. *After being released*, S. (who *remained* blindfolded) drew the impression of a figure which he had received. It was generally about as like the original as a child's blindfold drawing of a pig is like a pig; that is to say, it was a scrawl, but recognizable as intended to represent the original figure. In no case was there the smallest possibility that S. could have seen the original figure; and in no case did B. touch S., even in the slightest manner, while the figure was being drawn.

In one case, No. 6 in the series, the copy may be said to be as exact as S. could have drawn it blindfold if he had previously seen the original. The figures were not *reversed* on this day, as they had been on the previous one.

The whole series of figures (nine in number) are given in the accompanying plates. The number indicates the order in which they were drawn; the original drawing made by us is shown in the upper half of the plate, its reproduction by S. on the lower half.

No. 1.— Original Drawing.

No. 1.— Reproduction.

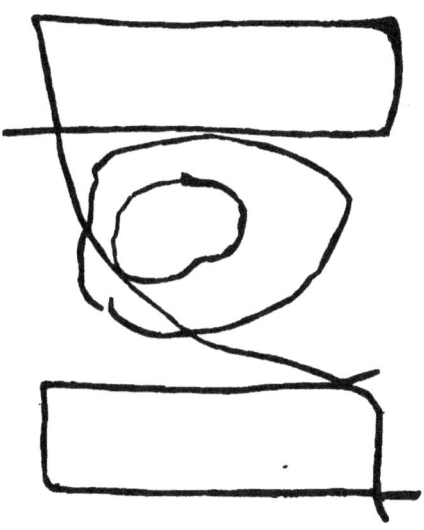

No. 2. — ORIGINAL DRAWING.

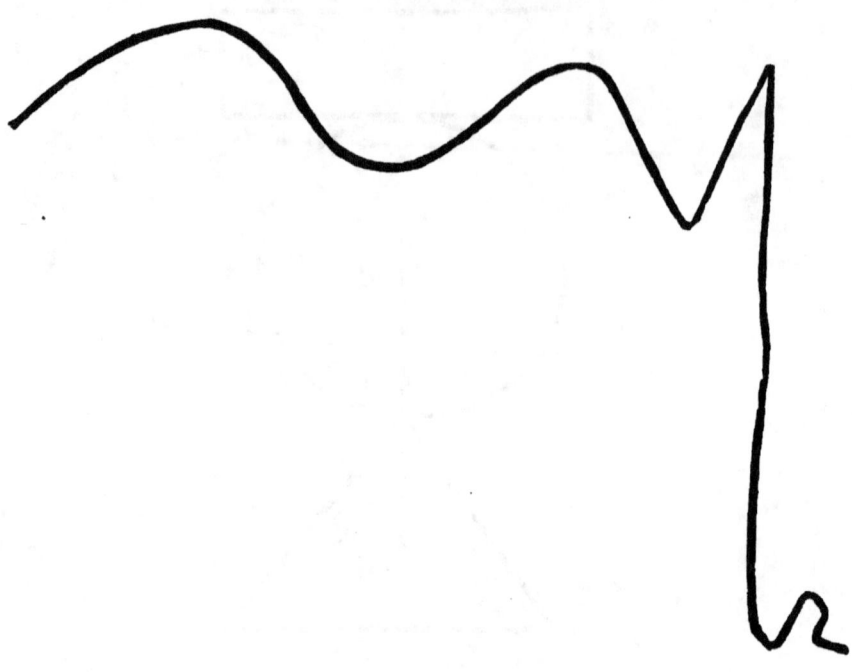

No. 2. — REPRODUCTION.

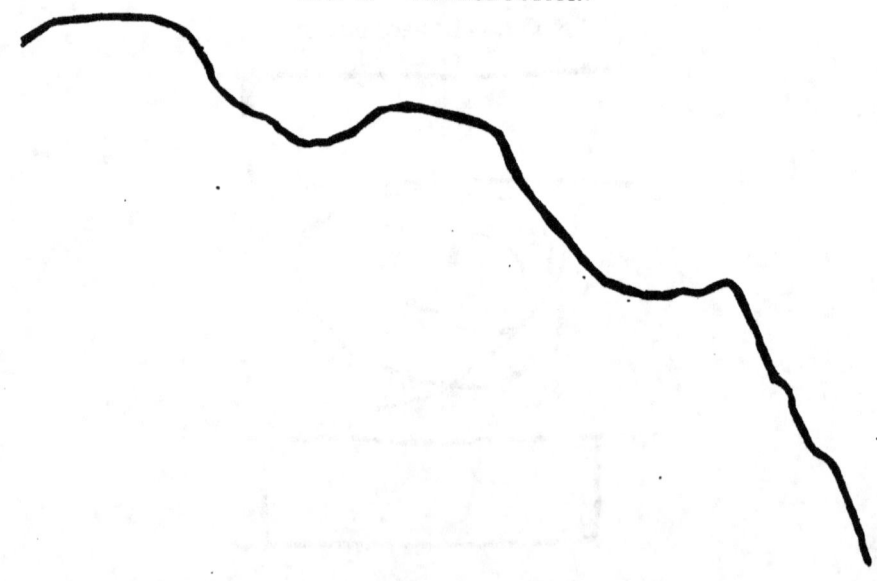

No. 3.—ORIGINAL DRAWING.

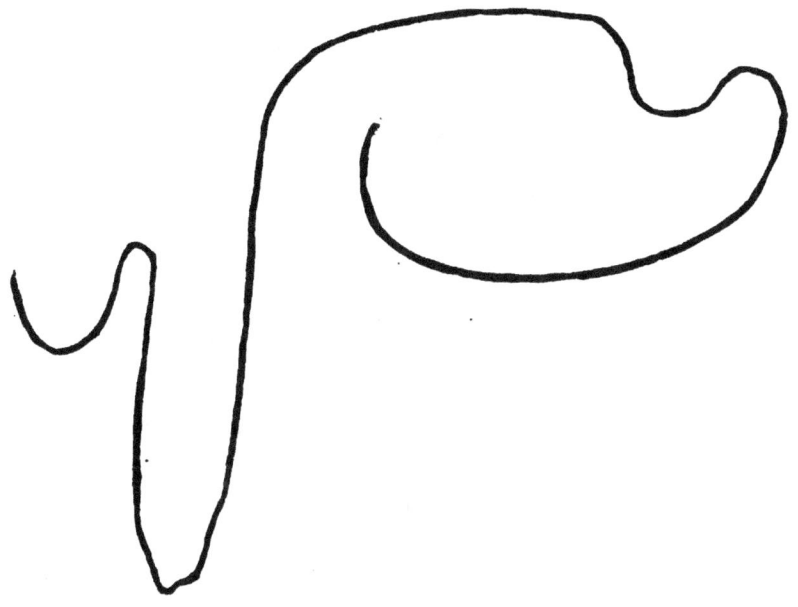

No. 3.—REPRODUCTION.

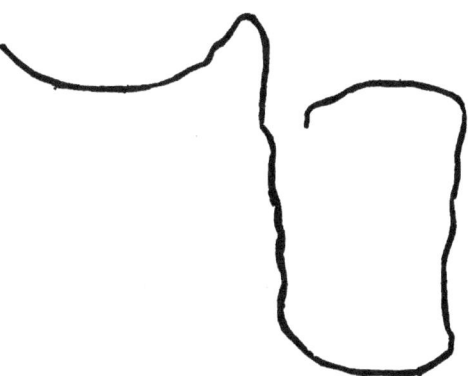

No. 4.—Original Drawing.

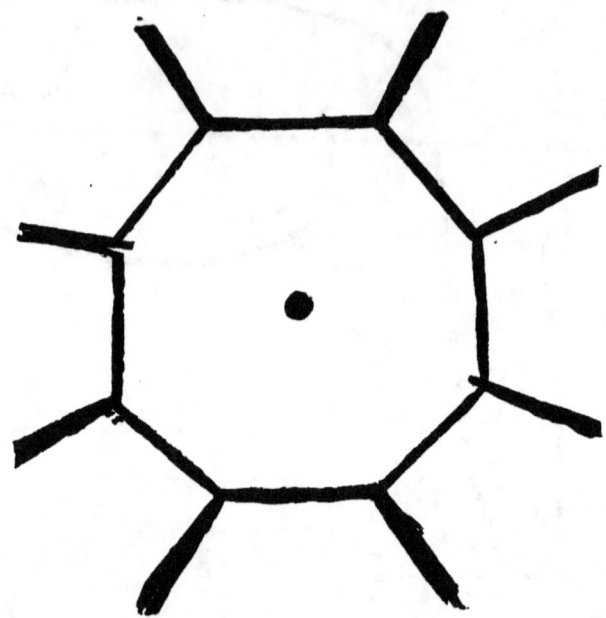

No. 4.—Reproduction.

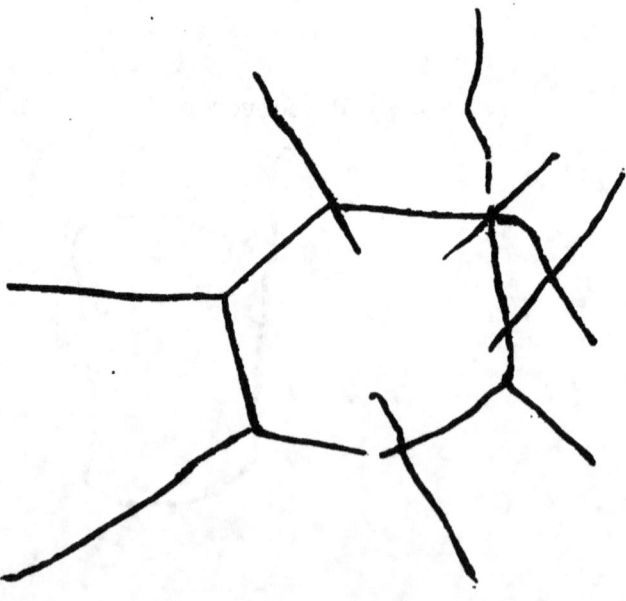

No. 5. — ORIGINAL DRAWING.

No. 5. — REPRODUCTION.

No. 6.—Original Drawing.

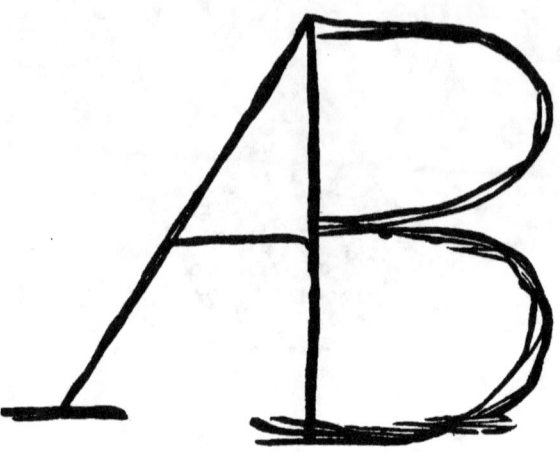

No. 6.—Reproduction.

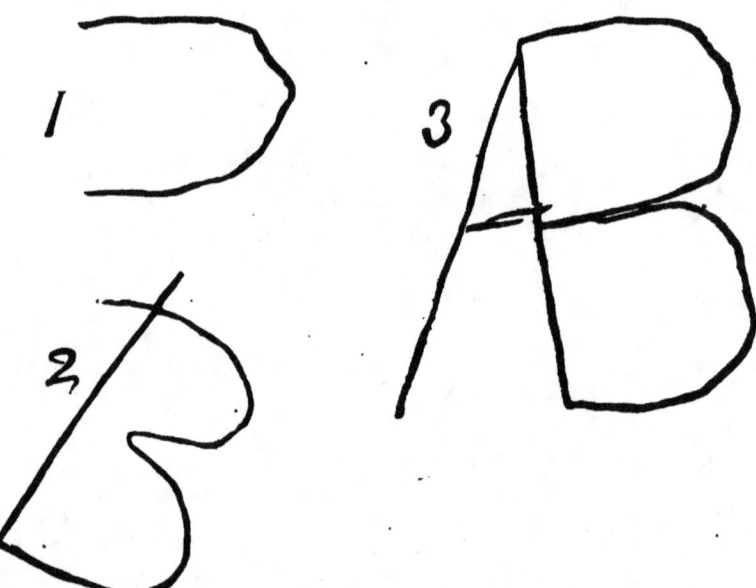

The figures in this and the next drawing indicate successive attempts, as if the mental picture were "glimpsed" piecemeal.

No. 7.—ORIGINAL DRAWING.

No. 7.—REPRODUCTION.

No. 8.—Original Drawing.

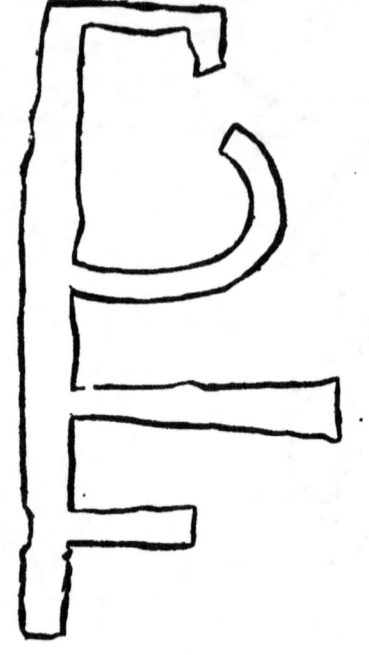

No. 8.—Reproduction.

No. 9.—Original Drawing.

No. 9.—Reproduction.

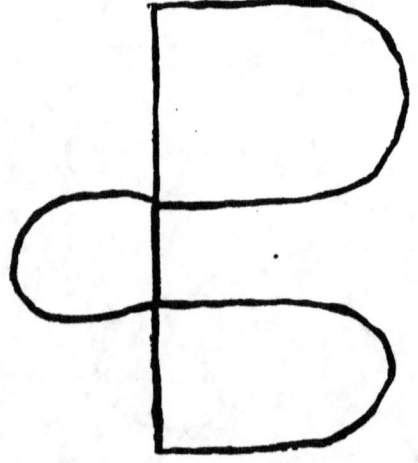

Mr. S. touched the spot to which the arrow points, and said: "There is something more there, but I cannot tell what it is."

IV.

˙On April 24, 1884, the Committee on Thought-Transference submitted a third Report. The committee had been enlarged, and consisted of Edmund Gurney, M.A., late Fellow of Trinity College, Cambridge; F. W. H. Myers, M.A., late fellow of Trinity College, Cambridge; F. Podmore, B.A., and Professor Barrett. The Report is as follows : —

At the close of the last Report a series of experiments were recorded, illustrating the reproduction of drawings without any discernible communication passing between the agent, Mr. Blackburn, who had momentarily seen the drawing made by one of us, and the percipient, Mr. G. A. Smith, who was blindfolded throughout the experiment. In these early experiments Mr. Smith held Mr. Blackburn's hand for a few moments, and then, releasing it, drew his impression of the figure. In this way we obtained a rough, but recognizable, reproduction of the nine figures which we had drawn. We have now to record a further extension of our inquiry in this direction, the experiments being made under conditions still more stringent than those at first imposed. We have also endeavored to ascertain how far the curious inversion of the figures, which had been noticed in the descriptions, but not in the pencil reproductions of the drawings, was accidental or otherwise.

At the invitation of the committee, Mr. Blackburn and Mr. Smith came from Brighton in January last, and met us at the rooms of the Society in Dean's Yard, where all the experiments about to be described were conducted. As Mr. Blackburn came only in answer to the urgent request of the committee, and at considerable inconvenience to himself, we feel it our duty to mention this fact, and, at the same time, to express our hearty obligations to him for the unrecompensed trouble which we have so frequently imposed upon him.

It is almost needless to point out that in these observations, so foreign to our common experience, it is indispensable to be minutely careful and conscientious in recording the exact conditions of each experiment. This we have striven to be ; and the reader will thus be enabled to form an independent judgment by making allowance for whatever mental bias he may discover in our conclusions. He has thus, moreover, the means afforded him of detecting possible errors, or of suggesting precautions which we may have overlooked.

Our *modus operandi* is as follows : The percipient, Mr. Smith, is seated blindfolded at a table in our own room ; a paper and pencil are within his reach, and a member of the committee is seated by his side. Another member of the committee leaves the room, and outside the closed door draws some figure at random. Mr. Blackburn, who, so far, has remained in the room with Mr. Smith, is now called out, and the door closed ; the drawing is then held before him for a few seconds, till its impression is stamped upon his mind. Then closing his eyes, Mr. Blackburn is led back into the room and placed standing or sitting behind Mr. Smith, at a distance of some two feet from him. A brief period of intense mental concentration on Mr. Blackburn's part now follows. Presently Mr. Smith takes up the pencil amidst the unbroken and absolute silence of all present, and attempts to reproduce on paper the inpression he has gained. He is allowed to do as he pleases as regards the bandage round his eyes ; sometimes he pulls it down before he begins to draw, but if the figures be not distinctly present to his mind, he prefers to let it remain on, and draws fragments of the figure as they are perceived. During all this time, Mr. Blackburn's eyes are, generally, firmly closed (sometimes he requests us to bandage his eyes tightly as an aid to concentration), and except when it is distinctly recorded, he has not touched Mr. Smith, and has not gone in front of him, or in any way within his possible field of vision, since he re-entered the room.[1]

[1] This precaution was not attended to in the experiments of one afternoon ; but these experiments, and these alone, are omitted from the series discussed below, as having been rendered nugatory through accidental circum-

When Mr. Smith has drawn what he can, the original drawing, which has so far remained outside the room, is brought in and compared with the reproduction. Both are marked by the committee and put away in a secure place. The drawings and reproductions given in this volume are in every case fac-similes of the untouched originals.

The experiments began on January 19, 1883, and were continued for three or four days in succession. During this series of experiments a considerable number of drawings were made, nearly all of which were exhibited at the following General Meeting. Another series of experiments were made in April. All the drawings may be seen at the Society's rooms; but it was thought unnecessary to reproduce the whole number. Those which are omitted, however, are by no means failures, and in fact only eight experiments, out of the total of thirty-seven, can be put down as unsuccessful, Mr. Smith in four cases failing to see anything, and in four cases giving so imperfect a representation that it might be called a failure. The first four figures were obtained after Mr. Blackburn had for a few minutes grasped Mr. Smith's hand — a procedure to which they were accustomed — as a supposed aid to Mr. Smith in visualizing Mr. Blackburn's mental picture. We, however, could allow no exception to our cardinal axiom on this subject, that no experiment where contact of any sort is allowed can be decisive; and though in the present instance the drawings were of such an irregular character that their description would have been extremely difficult to convey by imperceptible tracing or by any subtle code of pressure-signs, yet, assuming Mr. Blackburn and Mr. Smith to have been in collusion, the hypothesis was at least conceivable. Accordingly, we requested Mr. Blackburn to dispense altogether with the preliminary contact; and it must be understood that all the rest of the successful drawings (with the exception of two, not here reproduced, and of Fig. 13^{b} as explained) were done without any contact whatever, in the manner already indicated. Down

stances which were calculated to exercise, and obviously did exercise, a distracting effect on Mr. Blackburn's mind.

to Fig. 9 we had made rude geometrical drawings; at this point, one member of the committee, *without giving the least indication of his intention*, now drew Fig. 10 outside the room as usual. The grotesque reproduction by Mr. Smith is decidedly striking; and so also is the reproduction of the next figure, when Mr. Smith again apparently imagined that a geometrical figure had been drawn.

In some of the less accurate reproductions Mr. Blackburn complained of the difficulty he had in keeping the original drawing steadily in his mental view; and on one or two occasions we asked Mr. Blackburn to draw his recollection of the picture simultaneously with Mr. Smith (the two, of course, being kept out of sight of each other). We found that the main errors in Mr. Smith's reproduction existed already in Mr. Blackburn's recollection of the drawing. A striking illustration of this is given in Fig. 16, where the reproduction closely resembles Mr. Blackburn's drawing of what he remembered. It is, in fact, by no means easy to to keep vividly and correctly in mind for several minutes any irregular figure which has only been actually before the eye for a few seconds. We tried one experiment to test the effect of refreshing Mr. Blackburn's memory. Fig. 13 was drawn by us; and its reproduction, Fig. 13^a, was made by Smith in the usual way. The reproduction is very imperfect, being a sinuous, instead of a spiral line. No contact between the operators having so far occurred, we now asked Mr. Blackburn to touch Smith's hand for a few moments; on releasing it, the reproduction, 13^b, was obtained. Mr. Blackburn was now asked to stand (as at first) behind Mr. Smith, who remained blindfolded. The original drawing was now brought into the room, and held in front of Mr. Blackburn's eyes, and, therefore, some distance from the back of Smith's head. The latter now made the reproduction, 13^c, which is an exact copy of the original. We need hardly add that there were absolutely no means (such as mirrors, etc.) by which Smith, even if not blindfolded, could have gained any glimpse of the drawing, and, as we have already remarked, the most complete silence was preserved throughout these experiments.

We have now to consider whether it was possible that any information of the character of the designs drawn could have reached Smith through the ordinary avenues of sense. Of the five recognized gateways of knowledge, four — tasting, smelling, touch, and sight — were excluded by the conditions of the experiment. There remains the sense of *hearing*, which was but partially interfered with by the bandage over the eyes and ears. But the information can certainly not have been conveyed by speech ; our ears were as near to Mr. Blackburn as Mr. Smith's, and our eyes would have caught the slightest movement of his lips.

There remains the hypothesis of a code, consisting of audible signals other than oral speech ; and it would, no doubt, be an exaggeration to affirm that the possibility of such signals was absolutely excluded. We shall endeavor so to vary the conditions of subsequent experiments as to exclude this hypothesis completely : at present we will only point out the very great improbabilities which it involves, quite independently of our reliance on the integrity of Mr. Blackburn and Mr. Smith, which nothing has occurred to shake in the slightest degree.

Let our readers who may be familiar with the Morse or any other code of signals try in some such way to convey a description of some of our drawings to a friend who is blindfolded and has not seen the original ; we venture to assert that, even if audible signs were allowed, several minutes at least would be required to convey the notion of the figures correctly. It is probably no exaggeration to say that several scores, if not hundreds, of precise signs would be required to convey an idea as exact as that implied in many of Mr. Smith's representations. But in our experiments what sort of range existed for this mode of communication ! The material for possible signs appears to be reduced to shuffling on the carpet, coughing, and modes of breathing. Anything distinctly unusual in any of these directions must inevitably have been noticed ; and since our attention, during this part of the experiment, was of course concentrated on the relation between Mr. Blackburn and Mr. Smith we are at

a loss to conceive how any signalling. sufficient in amount to
convey the required ideas, could have passed undetected.
Furthermore, it must be observed that the reproductions were not
made in a tentative, hesitating manner as if waiting for signals ;
but deliberately and continuously, as if copying a drawing that is
seen. Moreover, in almost every instance the *proportions* of the
different parts of the original figure were reproduced more accurately than were its more easily describable details. However
with the view of removing all doubts that might arise as to possible auditory communications, we on one occasion stopped Mr.
Smith's ears with putty, then tied a bandage round his eyes and
ears, then fastened a bolster-case over the head, and over all
threw a blanket which enveloped his entire head and trunk.
Fig. 22 was now drawn by one of us, and shown outside the
room to Mr. Blackburn, who on his return sat behind Mr. Smith,
and in no contact with him whatever, and as perfectly still as it
is possible for a human being to sit who is not concentrating
his attention on keeping motionless to the exclusion of every
other object. In a few minutes Mr. Smith took up the pencil
and gave the successive reproductions shown below.

To profit by a code in this case, Mr. Smith would have had to
extract the putty from his ears unobserved by us (an action the
possibility of which the heavy swathings rendered just conceivable) and then, still smothered in bolster-case and blanket, to
detect periodic variations in Mr. Blackburn's breathing imperceptible to us ; to identify them as proceeding from Mr. Blackburn, and to interpret them into a description of the figure given
below. This hypothesis seems to us an extreme one, but, as
we have already said, we intend to meet it by yet further varying
and narrowing the conditions of future experiments.

We have now to describe some experiments which were undertaken to test whether the mental inversion of the object that had
been noticed in some of the early trials was accidental or otherwise. Mr. Smith, having been carefully blindfolded, sat with his
back to us, in a darkened room — some heavy opaque curtains
being between him and us. An arrow having been drawn on a
sheet of white paper, it was held by one of us in sight of Mr.

Blackburn, who remained in our presence, and sat facing the same way as Mr. Smith. In answer to the query, "How is the arrow pointing?" spoken by one of the Committee in a uniform tone of voice, Mr. Smith called out the direction as he mentally perceived it. We turned the arrow noiselessly, and at random, in different directions, and noted the following series of replies : —

TRUE POSITION OF ARROW.	POSITION AS STATED BY SMITH.
1. Pointing up	Pointing up.
2. " to left	" to right.
3. " down	" down.
4. " to right	" to right.
5. " up	" up.
6. " to left	" to right.
7. " up	" up.
8. " up	" up.
9. " up	" up.
10. " down	" down.
11. " to left	" down.
12. " to left	" down.
13. " up	" up.
14. " to right	" to left.
15. " to right	" to right.
16. " up	" up.
17. " up	" up.
18. " up	" up.
19. " to left	" to right.
20. " to right	" to left.
21. " down	" down.
22. " to right	" to right.
23. " to left	" to left.
24. " to left	" to right.
25. " up	" up.
26. " down	" down.
27. " up	" up.
28. " up	" up.

True Position of Arrow.	Position as Stated by Smith.
29. P'nting to left	P'nting to left.
30. " to right	" to left.
31. " up	" up.
32. " to right	" down.
33. " to right	" to left.
34. " down	" down.
35. " up	" up.
36. " to right	" to right.
37. " down	" down.
38. " to left	" down.
39. " up	" to right.
40. " down	" to right.
41. " to right	" to right.
42. " up	" up.

After the 37th trial Mr. Blackburn was obliged to leave; but we continued the experiments, one or two of the committee taking Mr. Blackburn's place, and with fair success. Counting these last, we made in all 42 trials. In these the arrow was held in a perpendicular position, up or down, 23 times; and of these cases 20 were guessed rightly, 3 wrongly. It was held in a horizontal position, right or left, 19 times; and of these cases 7 guessed rightly, 12 wrongly. The three wrong guesses when the arrow was in a perpendicular position occurred after Mr. Blackburn had left us; and in these cases the error was not one of inversion. Of the 12 wrong guesses, when the arrow was held horizontally, 8 were lateral inversions of the position of the arrow, as if it were seen in a mirror. Hence we see that 87 per cent of the answers were correct for the perpendicular position, and barely 37 per cent for the horizontal position; and, further, that it was about an even chance, when the arrow was horizontal, whether the image was described as laterally inverted or not.[1]

---

[1] Mr. Smith described the impression he obtained as that of a white arrow on a dark ground. We used at first an arrow drawn in ink on white paper. Without informing Mr. Smith (who remained behind the opaque curtain) of

[A number of pages of tabulated matter, and some deductions as to the possibilities of chance, are here omitted.]

It will, we think, be evident to any candid inquirer, who has carefully followed our investigations so far, that our experiments derive much strength and coherence from their very multitude and variety. In a question where the antecedent improbability of our conclusions seems so great, we could not be surprised if any single experiment — even an experiment in which sources of error were so completely excluded as in the cases where the Creery family correctly told cards, etc., unseen by anyone except the investigating committee — should leave the reader's mind still unconvinced. But we venture to assert that the *cumulative* character of the evidence which we have now amassed, and the extent to which we have eliminated the hypothesis of collusion, chance coincidence, and muscle or sign-reading, render our claim to have established the reality of this novel class of phenomena a very strong one. We continue carefully to consider all adverse criticism; but we venture to think that much of it really depends on an *à priori* presumption of impossibility which, natural though it may be, cannot, of course, be legitimately opposed to positive evidence.

The accompanying diagrams are facsimiles of the original drawings, which were obtained in the manner described. The accuracy of the engraving has been ensured by photographing the original drawings.

our intention, we cut an arrow out of white paper and placed it on a crimson cloth; Mr. Smith at once perceived the difference, and said he saw a kind of greenish arrow — this being (though *we* could hardly perceive it) the subjective color given to the arrow from its contiguity with the crimson cloth. We had no facilities at the moment for trying further experiments in this direction, and merely mention this result, which might have been accidental, as indicating another avenue of inquiry.

No. 1. — Original Drawing.

No. 1. — Reproduction.

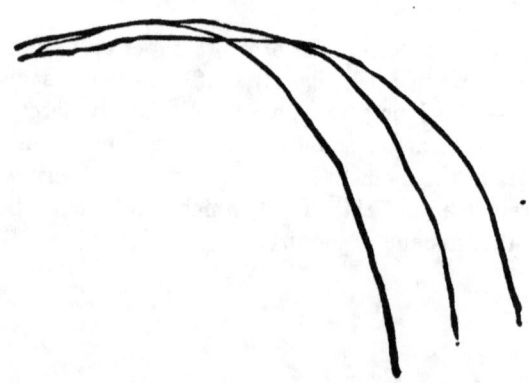

No. 2.—Original Drawing.

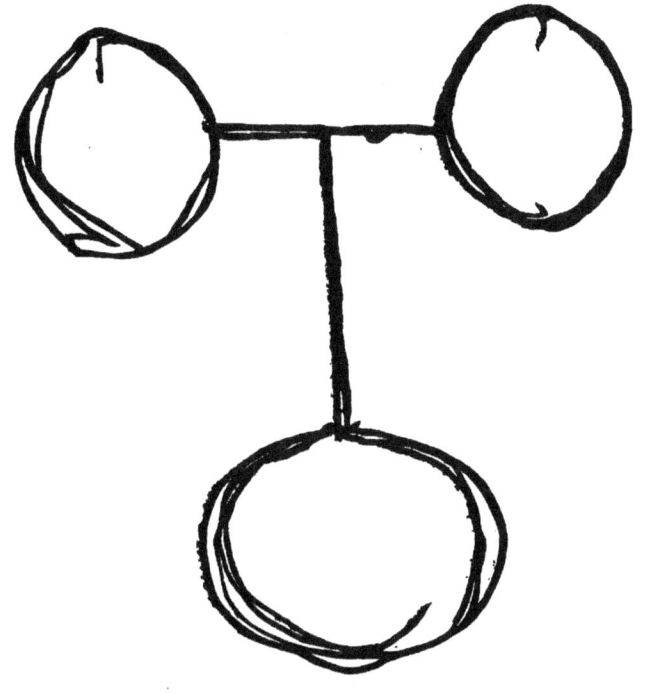

No. 2.—Reproduction.

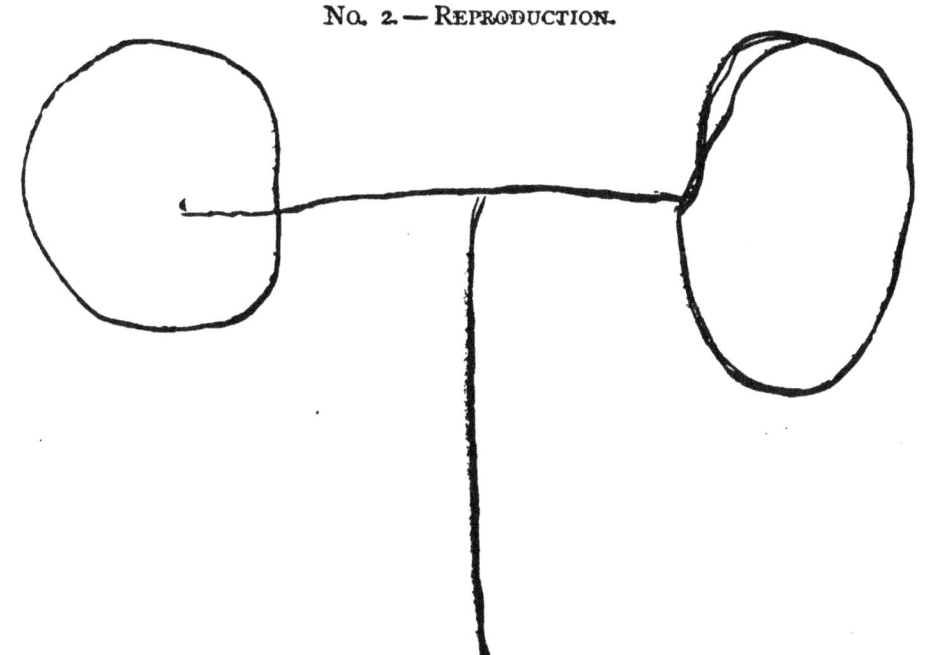

No. 3.—Original Drawing.

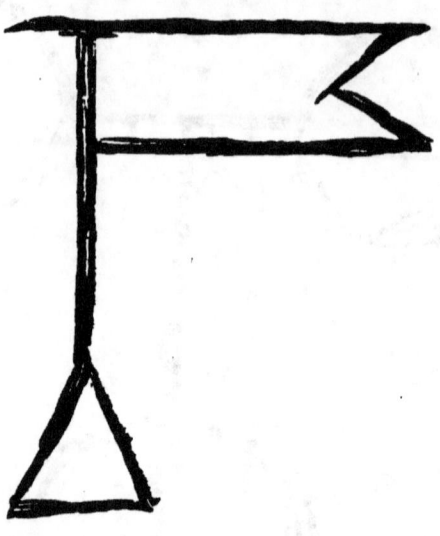

No. 3.—Reproduction.

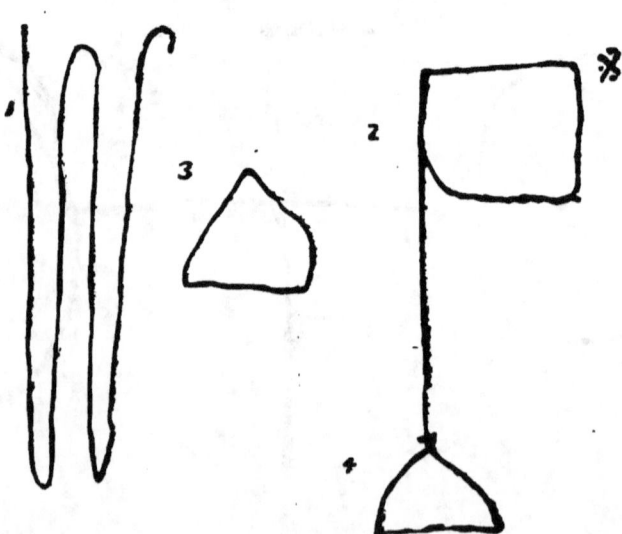

The figures indicate the order in which the drawings were made. At the close Mr. Smith said 1 should be "put on here somewhere," pointing to the spot where the asterisk is shown.

No. 4. — Original Drawing.

No. 4. — Reproduction.

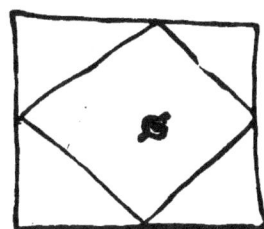

No. 5. — Original Drawing.   No. 5. — Reproduction.

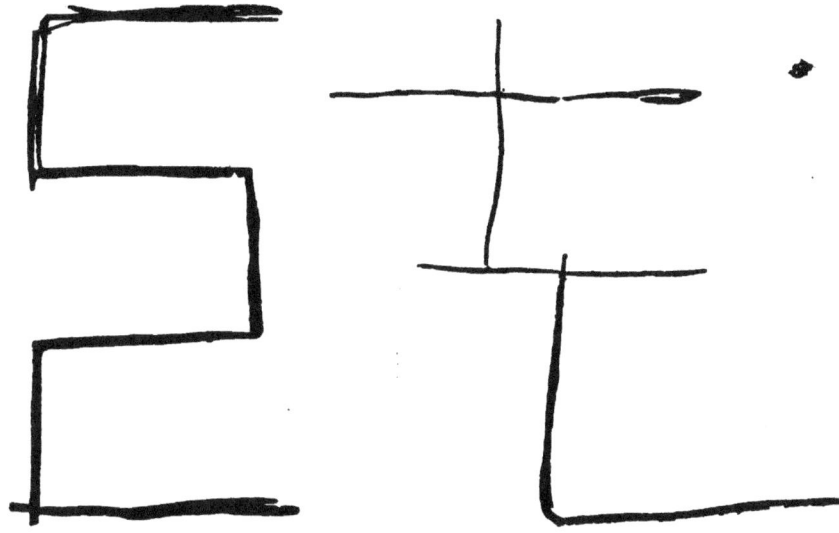

No. 6.—Original Drawing.

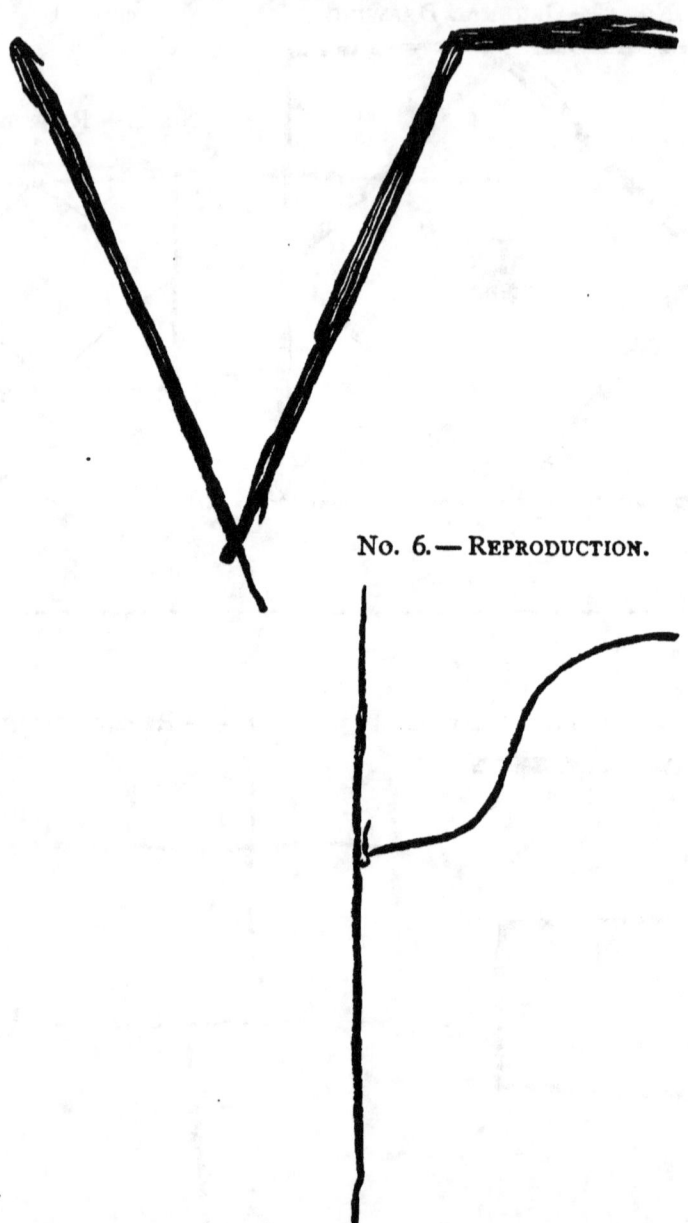

No. 6.— Reproduction.

After a brief period Mr. S. declared he could see nothing; his hands were then held by Mr. Blackburn for a few seconds, whereupon he declared that he saw "something like a sickle with the point resting on the ground." Fig. 6 (Reproduction) was then drawn.

No. 7. — Original Drawing.

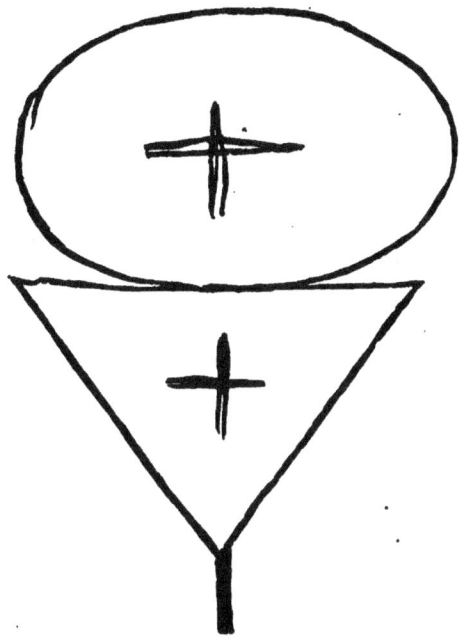

No. 7. — Reproduction.

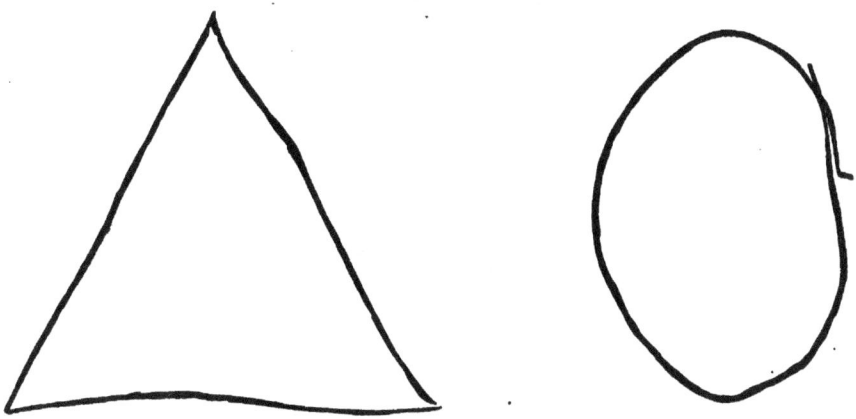

Mr. Smith said : " I can see a three-cornered thing, and there's a thing like a duck's egg somewhere." He mentioned afterwards that he had an impression of a cross right over the egg, and Mr. Blackburn said that he had found the cross against his will growing continually too large in his mental picture, and had once given up willing in the hope of reducing it.

No. 8.—Original Drawing.

No. 8.—Reproduction.

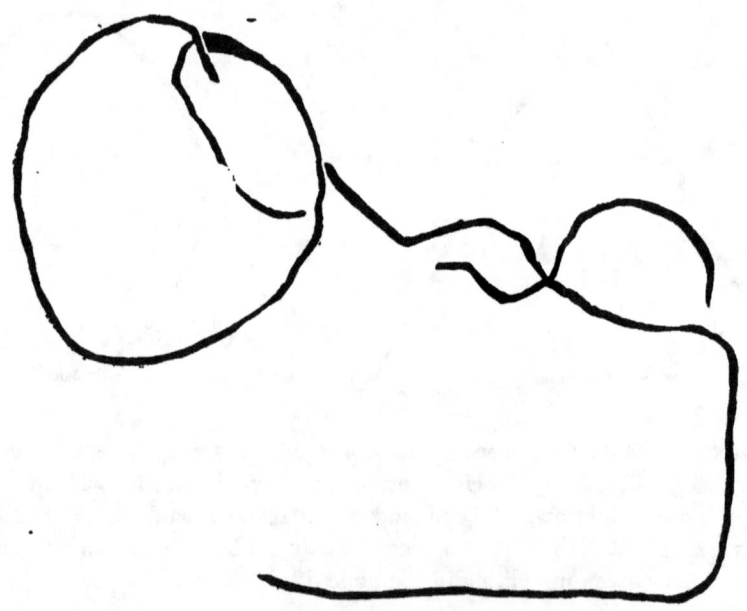

No. 9.—Original Drawing.

No. 9.—Reproduction.

No. 10. — Original Drawing.

No. 10. — Reproduction.

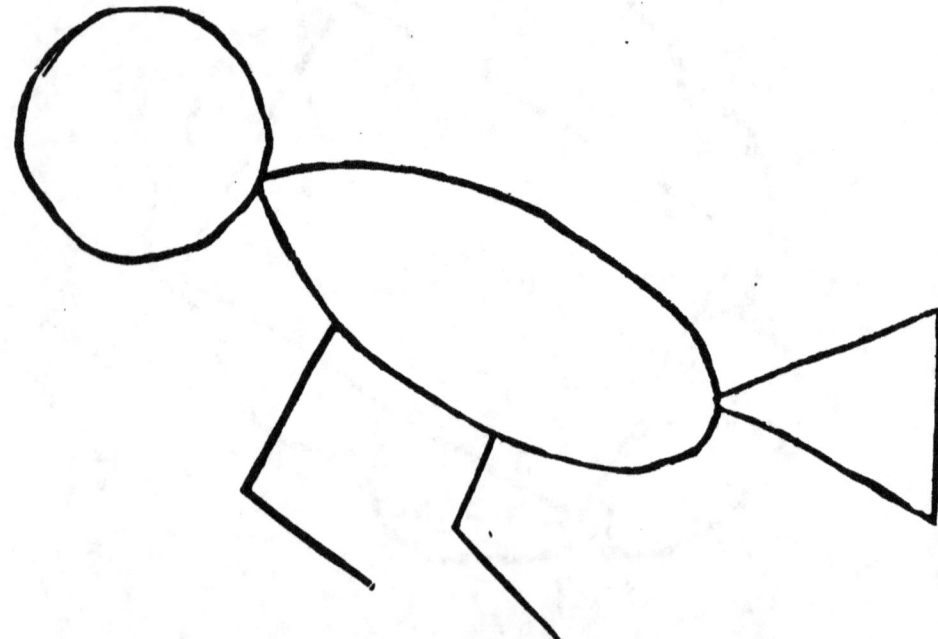

Mr. Smith had no idea that the original was not a geometrical drawing.

No. II. — ORIGINAL DRAWING.

No. II. — REPRODUCTION.

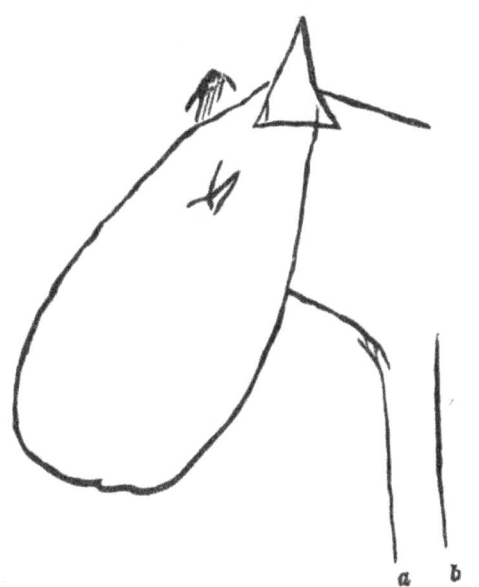

a　*b*

Mr. Smith had no idea that the original was not a geometrical diagram. He added line *b* some time after he had drawn line *a*, "seeing a line parallel to another somewhere."

No. 12. — ORIGINAL DRAWING.

No. 12. — REPRODUCTION.

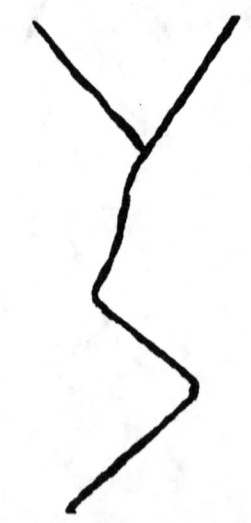

No. 13.— Original Drawing.   No. 13*a*. — Reproduction.

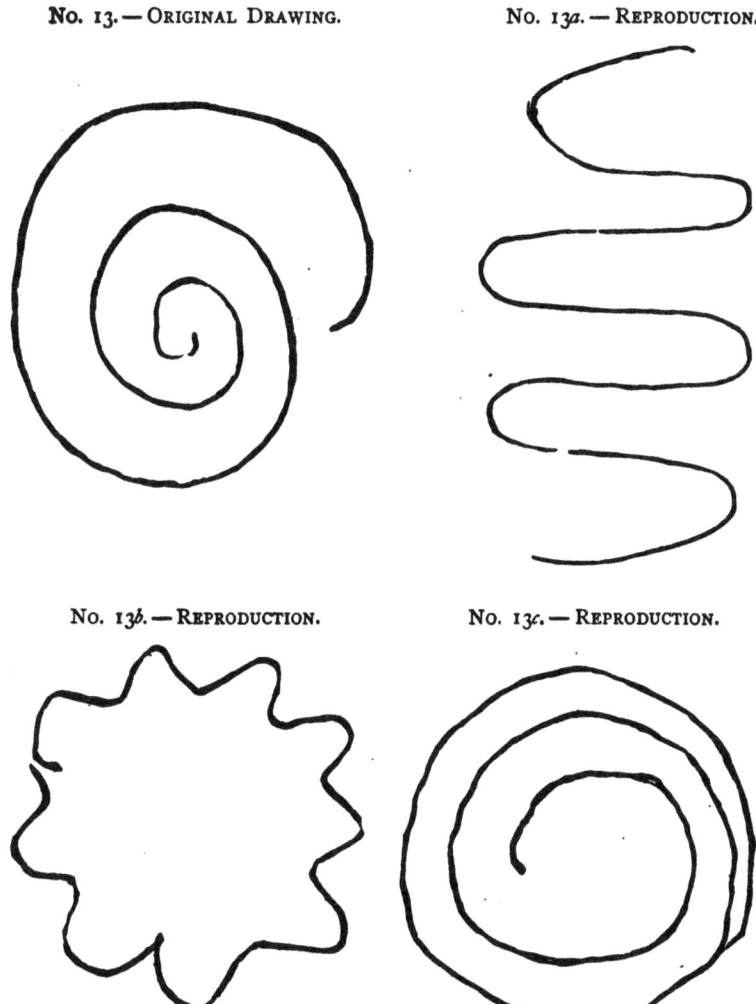

No. 13*b*. — Reproduction.   No. 13*c*. — Reproduction.

No. 13*b* was made after Mr. Blackburn had momentarily held Mr. Smith's hand ; No. 13*c* after Mr. Blackburn had refreshed his memory by again looking at the original.

No. 14.—Original Drawing.

No. 14.—Reproduction.

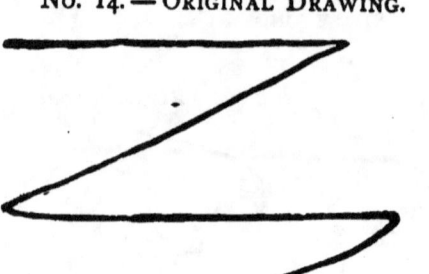

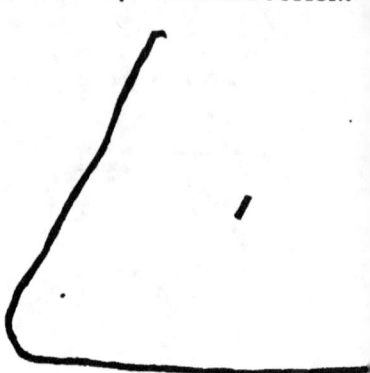

No. 14.—Reproduction.

No. 14.—Reproduction.

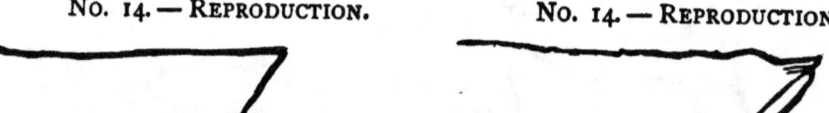

No. 15. — Original Drawing.

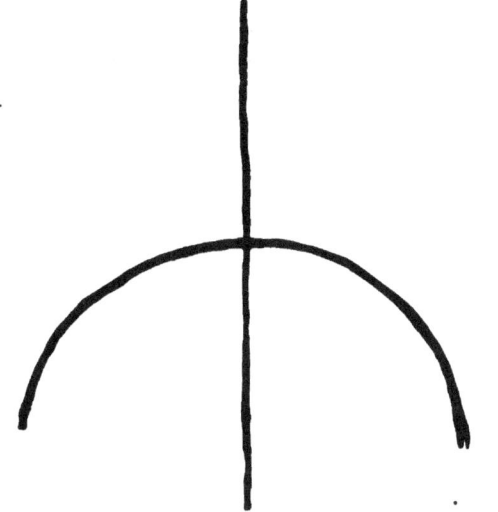

No. 15. — Reproduction.

No. 16.—Original Drawing.

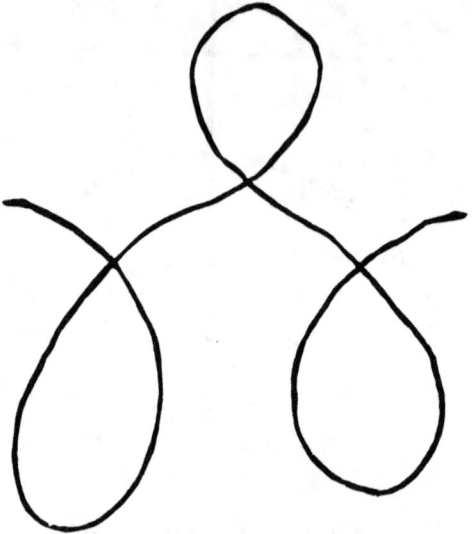

No. 16.—Reproduction.

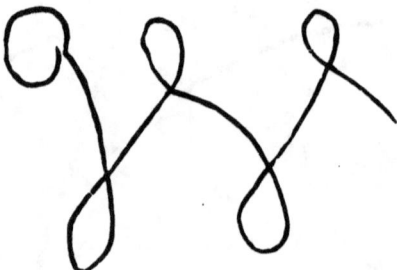

Mr. Blackburn had not precisely remembered the figure, and drew the following as representing what he had in his mind.

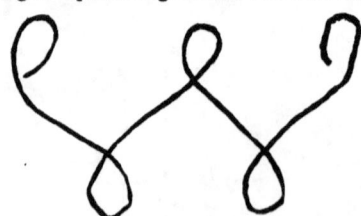

No. 17.—ORIGINAL DRAWING.

No. 17.—REPRODUCTION.

Inner circle begun at point marked +, and then carried round in one continuous line from left to right.

No. 18.—Original Drawing.

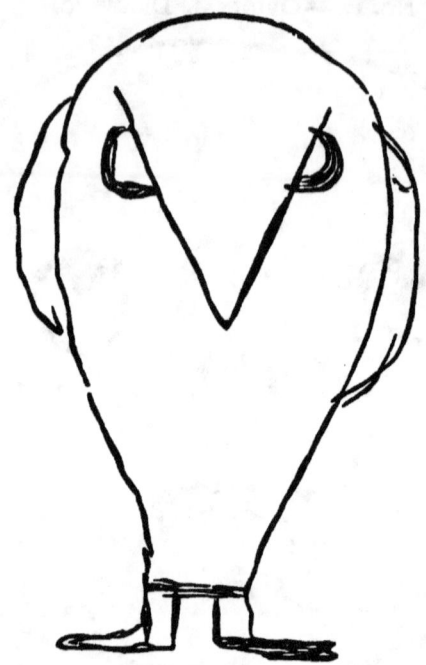

No. 18.—Reproduction. 1.   No. 18.—Reproduction. 2.

 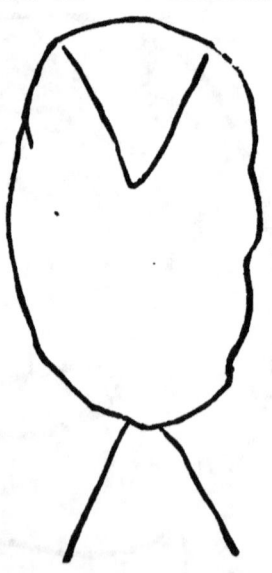

Mr. Blackburn forgot the eyes.

No. 19.—Original Drawing.

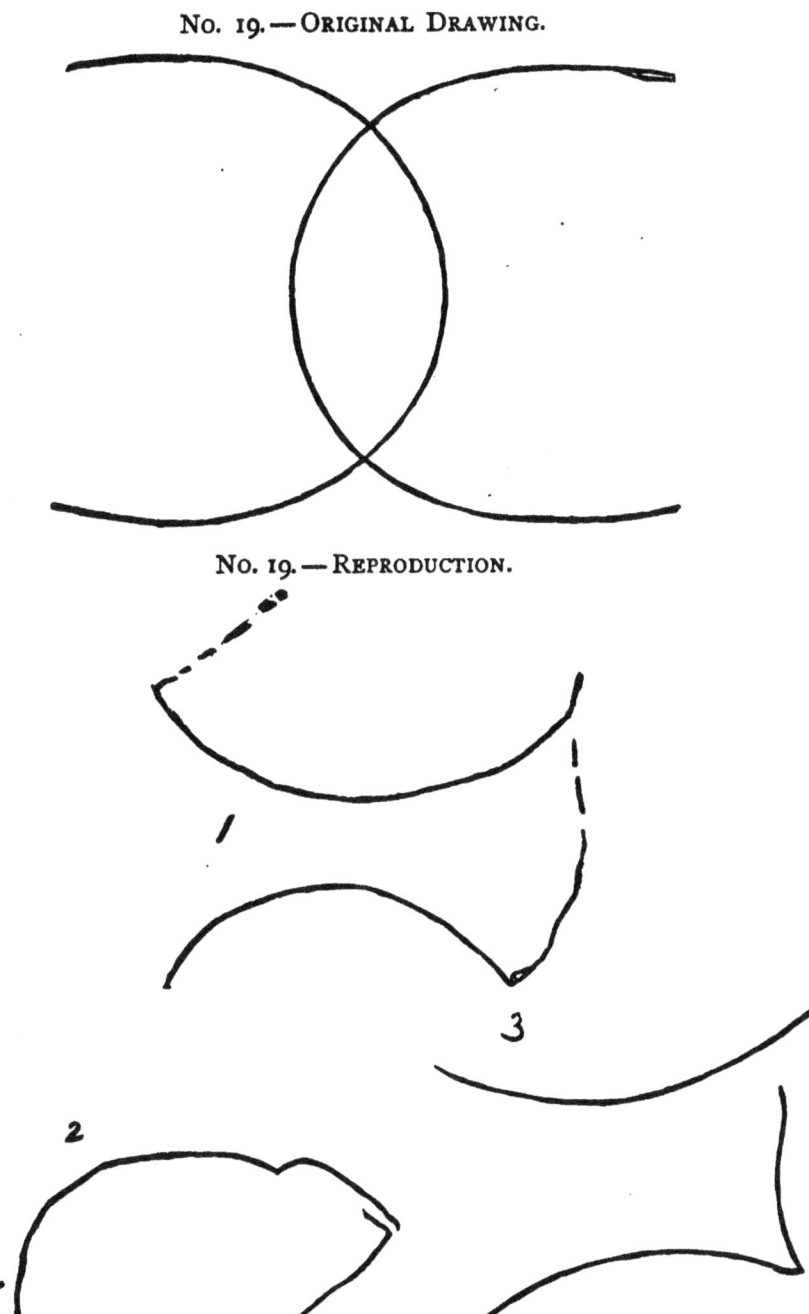

No. 19.—Reproduction.

Mr. Blackburn was fixing his mind on the oval, in order
to make Mr. Smith connect the lines he had got.

No. 20.—ORIGINAL DRAWING.

No. 20.—REPRODUCTION.

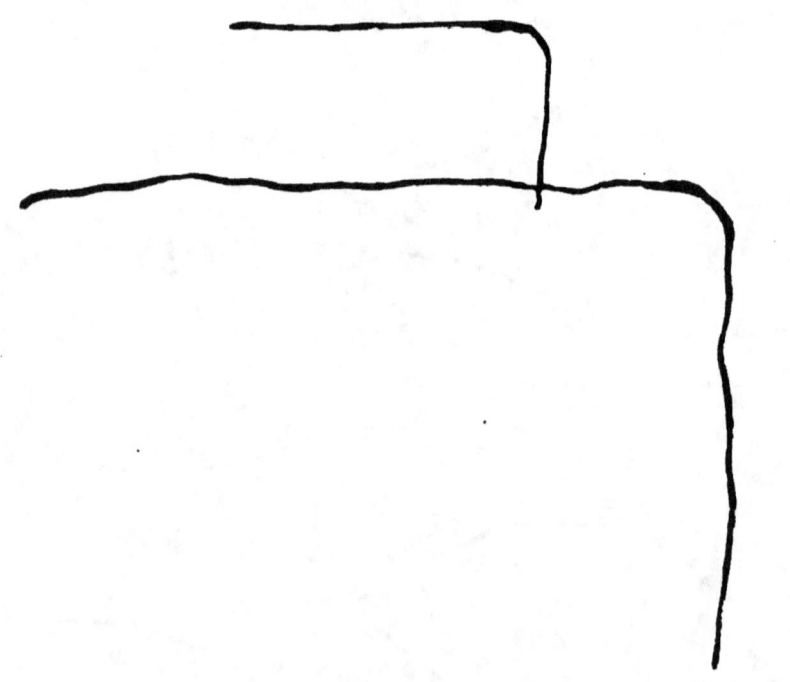

No. 21.—Original Drawing.

No. 21.—Reproduction.

Mr. Blackburn was imagining the handles as turned *outwards*.

No. 22. — Original Drawing.

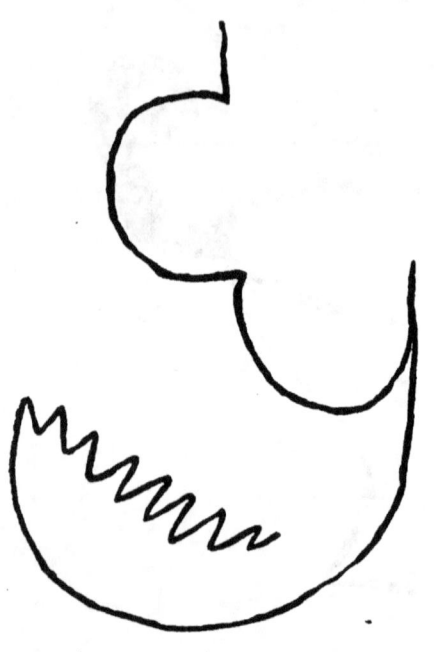

No. 22. — Reproduction.

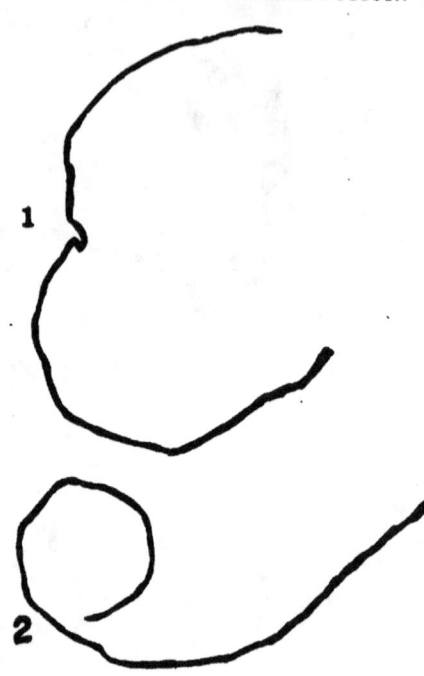

No. 22. — Reproduction.

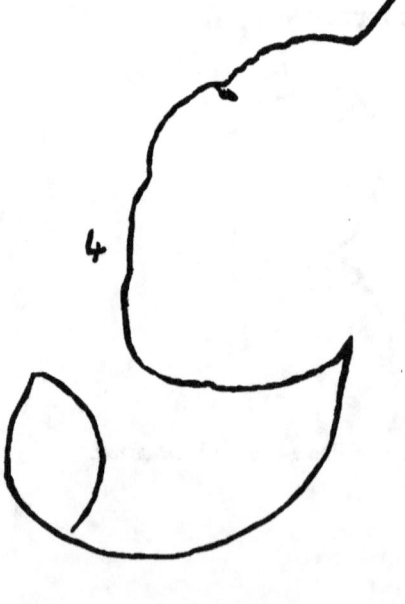

No. 22. — Reproduction.

V.

At the meeting of the Society held Nov. 22, 1883, Mr. Guthrie submitted a report which is specially interesting, as showing how he was led to investigate the subject, as well as additional results obtained. He says : —

After Mr. Irving Bishop's visit to Liverpool in the spring of this year, it became a favorite amusement to imitate his skill in pin-finding ; and some persons also made experiments in reading numbers thought of by others, they themselves meanwhile being blindfolded. Out of experiments made in this casual way arose the systematic study which it is my business to recount in the present paper. A party of young ladies amusing themselves after business hours found that certain of their number, when blindfolded, were able to name very correctly figures selected from an almanac suspended on the wall of the room, when their companions, having hold of their hands, fixed their attention upon some particular day of the month. There, so far as the young ladies were concerned, the matter ended. They had their few evenings' amusement, and other occupations and interests supervened.

It so happened that about this time I read an article by Mr. F. Corder in the February number of "Cassell's Magazine," which was written with such an air of truthfulness, and spoke of thought-transference as a matter of such very ordinary experience, that for the first time I began to think that there must be some foundation in fact for the belief so confidently expressed. Up to that time I had been thoroughly skeptical, nor had I read any literature on the subject. I thereupon determined to try the experiments, as described in Mr. Corder's paper, upon my son, a nervous and susceptible fair-haired boy of ten years of age. Much to my astonishment and his own, he named quickly and without difficulty objects which I placed behind him when blindfolded under the usual conditions. He, however, would not perform more than two or three experiments at a time, saying that it made him "feel queer." Moreover, after the first experiments, when I asked others to witness the curious phenomenon, he seemed disposed to ensure success by taking a sly peep at the object, which indeed made me suspicious of the whole thing. Under these circumstances of the boy's reluctance, and the difficulty of imposing stringent conditions, I abandoned him as an unsuitable subject for study, more particularly as other satisfactory means shortly afterwards came under my notice. I, however, at a subsequent period, tested my son's powers under proper scientific conditions with the assistance of Mr. Birchall; and we were both satisfied as to his possession of the faculty, although we did not consider him a useful subject for study.

It was after the discovery of my son's powers of receiving impressions that I heard of the casual experiments before referred to; and having tested the accuracy of the reports which I had received, I mentioned the matter to the Council of the Literary and Philosophical Society of Liverpool, asking for assistance for the purpose of a scientific study of the phenomena. Mr. James Birchall, the honorary secretary, to whom the subject was quite new, having, I suppose, some confidence in my good judgment, agreed to give me the advantage of his assistance, and we thereupon held our first meeting. From the very beginning it was arranged between us that Mr. Birchall should make a full and complete record of every experiment, and I have to tender him my grateful thanks for the exactitude and care with which this record has been kept. He has performed his office as a man free from any prepossessions, and simply as a matter of official duty. His suggestions have all been in the direction of stringency of conditions, and I may state that he very shortly became convinced of the *bona fides* of the experiments, and interested in the scientific prosecution of the study. I very much regret that he is not able to be present at this meeting, as we had arranged, in order personally to present the valuable and interesting register of the experiments which he has prepared. I hope, however, that he will be able to attend some future meeting with a report upon experiments which we are continuing week by week.

And now as to the party of young ladies to whom I referred as having discovered the possession of the power of thought-transference. You must know that I am a partner in one of the large drapery establishments in the city of Liverpool, and that the young ladies are connected with one of the show-rooms of that establishment. A relative of mine (entered in Mr. Birchall's report as Miss C.), also in the business, had been present at the careless, off-hand experiments made in imitation of Irving Bishop, and, recognizing their genuine character, informed me of the circumstance, being aware of the experiments I had made with my son.

One of the most important considerations connected with my study has been that I have been made cognizant, through this relative, of the very beginnings of the affair. I have, as it were, been behind the scenes from the first, and, through my representative, have been informed of almost every experiment which has been made outside our weekly meetings, — although after the first month the young ladies agreed only to practise at these meetings, as I (rightly or wrongly) thought it desirable on considerations of health to limit their work in this direction. Thus I have had the advantage of studying a series of experiments *ab ovo*. I had not to enter upon an examination of the achievements of people who had been working together for years; but have been acquainted with the origin and whole development of the manifestations, and have witnessed the genuine surprise which the operators and the subjects have alike exhibited at their increasing successes, and at the results of our excursions into novel lines of experiment. The affair has not been the discovery of the possession of special powers, first made and then worked up by the parties themselves for gain or glory. The experimenters in this case were disposed to pass the matter over altogether as one of no moment, and only put themselves at my disposal in regard to experiments in order to oblige me. The experiments have all been devised and conducted by myself and Mr. Birchall without any previous intimation of their nature, and could not possibly have been foreseen. In fact they have been to the young ladies a succession of surprises. No set of experiments of a similar nature has ever been more completely known from its origin, or more completely under the control of the scientific observer.

As to the young ladies concerned, I have known them all for many years, and am able to speak in the highest terms of their probity and intelligence. I know also that they have a high regard for me, and would not willingly lead me into any error.

The two subjects, Miss R. and Miss E., are about twenty years of age, engaged in business all day from 9 A.M. to 6 P.M., in the same show-room, and they discovered their aptitude with their companions in the same room as operators or agents. They do not meet elsewhere, as all the assistants live with their friends, and do not board on the establishment. The lady, Miss R——d, who is supposed to have the principal influence in conveying impressions, is the head of the room, and occupies a position of great trust and responsibility.

The experiments were commenced with simple shapes, such as diamonds, circles, triangles, etc., cut out of brightly-colored ribbons, and exhibited upon a black background; also with cards and letters of the alphabet printed in a bold type. Afterwards objects were introduced, and short words were formed of the letters. The first series of experiments were of a *visual* kind, and were very successful. They were conducted in the presence of Mr. Birchall, myself, several lady companions of the subjects, and usually one or two members of the Literary and Philosophical Society. In the earlier experiments the subject was in contact (that is to say clasped or touched hands) with Miss R——d or some other lady friend. I need not say that the subject was always effectually blindfolded, and that the object was placed in such a position that it could not be seen by her, even if she were not so incapacitated for observation. These conditions apply to all the experiments, and, to save iteration, I state them once for all.

After a short time, experiments of this description were performed without any contact whatever. This was a suggestion of my relative, and, under her superintendence, the first set of experiments with Miss R., under these new conditions, was com- pletely successful, and will be found recorded in Mr. Birchall's report. At the next meeting after this discovery, the experi- ments were tried without contact, and were almost uniformly successful. The party sat in a semicircle before Miss R. or Miss E., the object being placed behind her, and, the attention of all being concentrated upon it, the object was very speedily described and sometimes named. It is noteworthy that the idea or name of the object did not come first to the percipient, but the appearance seemed to dawn gradually upon the mind, and sometimes it only presented itself in its general features, so that very often it could only be described and not named. First the color impression was received, then the general shape, and after- wards any special characteristic, and finally, the name. This was the usual order of the process. As an illustration, take the case of a blue feather. The subject said, "It is pale. It looks like a leaf; but it can't be a leaf — looks like a feather curled. Is it a feather?" Again, a key was described as "A little tiny thing with a ring at one end and a little flag at the other, like a toy flag." Urged to name it, she said, "It is very like a key."

The foregoing is a summary of our work during the first few weeks. All our regular meetings were successful, but in our desire to exhibit our discovery to our fellow members, we had some extra meetings, which proved total failures, much to our chagrin, and much to the disappointment of our subjects. It would appear that any mental disturbance on the part of the operators or on the part of the subjects, due to anxiety to succeed, or to the novelty of the *entourage* of persons or things, very much interferes with the success of experiments. I may here remark that the result of our experience is that success or failure depends as much (if not more) upon the condition of the agent as upon that of the percipient. It has happened that, after a complete failure before strangers, the agent and percipi- ent have been almost immediately able to obtain a successful transference of a number of impressions — the previous failure having been probably due to the mind of the agent occupying itself with the presence of the visitor, instead of being directed exclusively upon the object to be described. As regards the condition of the agent, I may say that although I have been very successful myself in giving impressions to each of the subjects, without the presence of any other person, still, under precisely similar conditions, when I have not felt equal to the required effort of concentration, I have been unable to repeat the success. We have also found that wandering attention on the part of the agents is misleading; and it would, I think, be fair to explain in this way one or two failures of the following type — that although a certain article was placed for observation, a picture hanging on the wall a little above it was described. On account of the disturbance of the agent's mind, as well as that of the subject, it is judged that experiments in a drawing-room, before a large miscellaneous company, are not likely to be successful.

At the conclusion of the first series of experiments some new departures were made.

First we tried the experiment of producing an article in the absence of the subject from the room, and after concealing it readmitting her, and after blindfolding and isolating her asking her to describe the object we had been looking at. This experiment was tried both before and after the summer interregnum, and was successful. Thus a lady's purse, in form of a satchel, with a bright metallic frame and steel bar handle above, was thus described: " Is it something not quite square? Something bright in the middle. Is it a purse? There is something very bright at the top. Has it anything else over it? Don't know what this is — whether it belongs to the purse. I've lost it — is it a bag?" On another occasion a key was correctly named, and Mr. John-son's gold watch-chain, hanging in a curve from his watch-pocket to a button-hole of his waistcoat, elicited the answer: " Is it a chain, a watch-chain, hanging from a pocket like this?" the percipient then describing in the air a curve similar to that formed by the chain we had been looking at, but which was now concealed. Then she added, " There is a little pendant at the end of it."

Proceeding a step further we agreed, in the absence of the subject from the room, to imagine some object, and, under similar conditions, to ask her to describe it. This experiment was also successfully performed, on several occasions, by both subjects. A gold cross, pine-apple, and other objects imagined in this way have been correctly named.

We tried also the perception of *motion*, and found that the movements of objects exhibited could be discerned. .The idea was suggested by an experiment tried with a card which, in order that all present should see, I moved about, and was informed by the percipient, Miss R., that it was a card, but she could not tell which one, because it seemed to be moving about. On a subsequent occasion, in order to test this perception of motion, I bought a toy monkey, which worked up and down on a stick by means of a string drawing the arms and legs together. The answer was : " I see red and yellow, and it is darker at one end than the other. It is like a flag moving about — it is moving. . . . Now it is opening and shutting like a pair of scissors."

We have also tried experiments in the transference of real or imaginary *pains*, which Miss R. is able to receive from Mr. Birchall. This branch of our studies has not as yet been carried very far, for want of time, although I think it more likely to throw light upon the nature of the mode of transmission than any other branch of the inquiry. In particular, it would be desirable to ascertain, by observation or even experiment, if the part affected in the subject shows signs of physical change, such as contraction, tension, rush of blood, redness, or any other physical change similar to that produced upon the person of the agent in causing the pain.

At the conclusion of our spring session, we tried (without contact) the transference of names, short quotations, &c., all the company thinking of the word or words. In this we met with but little success, but on one occasion, the proverb. " Time flies," having been thought of by the company, elicited the answer, " Is , it two words ? — is it ' Time flies ' ? "

On this occasion, seeing that the subject was so apt, I proposed to the company that we should think of a historical scene, and two experiments were made, which are published in Mr. Birchall's report. They were imperfect, viewed critically, each of them having been done at the second instead of at the first attempt; but if the fact of thought-transference is accepted as proved on other grounds, they are suggestive of further experiments in the same direction.

We discontinued our experiments at the end of May, on account of press of business and arrangements for holidays; and I am told by the subjects that no experiments whatever were made until we resumed our meetings, towards the end of August, in preparation for a visit by Mr. Myers and Mr. Gurney. As I expected, after the interregnum we met with very little success, and I wrote to those gentlemen not to expect much under the circumstances. And, indeed, the "subjects" were able to do very little, and our visitors would have gone away disappointed, had not our inquiries taken the direction of experiments in transference of *tastes*.

I may add the results of a few casual experiments, made in the course of the last week in London, which illustrate the partial transference of somewhat more complex visual impressions than most of those above described.

One evening I called Miss E. and a friend of mine, Mr. Lee, out of the room, and requested them to assist me in imagining the large stained glass rose-window in the transept of Westminster Abbey, opposite to which Miss E., Miss R., and I had been sitting at the service the same afternoon. I then asked Miss R. to say what object we were thinking of. After a while she said, " I cannot tell what you are looking at, but I seem to be sitting in Westminster Abbey, where we were this afternoon." After another interval, she said, " I seem to be looking at a window," and again, " I think it is the window in the chancel with the figures." When afterwards told which window it was, she said that she did not see any window distinctly, and certainly not the rose-window thought of.

I next proposed another object, and decided upon something

which had struck our attention in a lamp shop in New Bond Street, a lighted lamp with a stuffed monkey clinging to it — the lamp at the same time revolving, and the monkey moving a cocoanut, which was suspended from its foot. This experiment took a very long time, and was only partially successful. First Miss R. said she thought of a cat, or it might be a dog. After a while she said it was something long, dark, and hanging — describing the size and shape pretty well with her hands. Then she said that she saw something hanging straight down, and moving up and down. After the removal of the blindfolding, she looked at the gas chandelier, and said, " Was it not that? " and then immediately, " No, it was not that — it was a lamp, and it was lighted." Asked if the cat she saw had anything to do with the lamp, she said, " No."

The following completely successful results in the simpler forms of thought-transference were also obtained on the same occasion as the above.

I proposed to Miss R. to tell a name thought of by myself, Mr. Lee, and Miss E., without contact and blindfolded. The name " Polly " was written on a card and passed round in strict silence. In a few minutes Miss R. said, " I can only think of Polly."

The name " Isabella " was then selected by me, and passed round silently. After a longer interval, Miss R. said, " I don't know what it can be. Somehow I can only think of my own name." Asked what was her name, she said, " Isabel."

Mr. Lee proposed thinking of a number, and as only single numbers had previously been thought of, it occurred to me to take a double one — 34 — which I wrote down and passed round. Miss R. shortly said, " Are there two figures ? " I said " Yes." " One is 4 and the other 3." She did not know whether it was 34 or 43.

Our endeavors recently have been towards the ascertainment of individual powers on the part of the agents in regard to each of the two subjects. The test selected has been the production, by the blindfolded subjects, of copies of drawings placed behind them. An improved method has been to place the drawing on a stand, with a wooden back between the agent and the subject, and the agent, placing himself on the opposite side of a small table, either joins hands with the subject, or, by preference, does not touch her at all, and gazes at the drawing until the subject says she has an impression thereof. The drawing is then taken down and concealed, the blindfolding is removed, and the subject, being already provided with drawing materials, proceeds to delineate the impression she has received. In most of these cases no one besides the agent and the subject has been present in the room, and the result is held to establish the relative power of each agent in giving off an impression of this kind. In this way it has been found that all the agents have been successful in giving information individually to each of the subjects, although the range of experiments is not yet complete, because some new operators we have introduced have not yet had time to develop or settle down properly to their work. However, it has been found that both Miss R. and Miss E. have been able to receive impressions of drawings singly from myself, Mr. Birchall, Miss R —— d, Mr. Steel, President of the Literary and Philosophical Society of Liverpool, and imperfectly from two or three other gentlemen. Since my arrival in London, a very successful producer of impressions has been discovered in the person of one of your members, Mr. F. S. Hughes. Mr. Gurney was also successful at one of our meetings.

The originals of the following diagrams were for the most part drawn in another room from that in which the subject was placed. The few executed in the same room were drawn while the subject was blindfolded, at a distance from her, and in such a way that the process would have been wholly invisible to her or any one else, even had an attempt been made to observe it. During the process of transference, the agent looked steadily and in perfect silence at the original drawing, which was placed upon an intervening wooden stand; the subject sitting opposite to him, and behind the stand, blindfolded and quite still. The agent ceased looking at the drawing, and the blindfolding was removed, only when the subject professed herself ready to make the reproduction, which happened usually in times varying from half a minute to two or three minutes. Her position rendered it absolutely impossible that she should glimpse at the original. She could not have done so, in fact, without rising from her seat and advancing her head several feet; and as she was almost in the same line of sight as the drawing, and so almost in the centre of the agent's field of observation, the slightest approach to such a movement must have been instantly detected. The reproductions were made in perfect silence, and without the agent even following the actual process with his eyes, though he was of course able to keep the subject under the closest observation.

In the case of all the diagrams, except those numbered 7 and 8, the agent and the subject were the only two persons in the room during the experiment. In the case of numbers 7 and 8, the agent and subject were sitting quite apart in a corner of the room, while Mr. Guthrie and Miss E. were talking in another part of it. Numbers 1–6 are specially interesting as being the complete and consecutive series of a single sitting.

No. 1.—Original Drawing.   No. 1.—Reproduction.

Mr. Guthrie and Miss E.   No contact.

No. 2.—Original Drawing.   No. 2.—Reproduction.

Mr. Guthrie and Miss E.   No contact.

No. 3. — Original Drawing.

No. 3. — Reproduction.

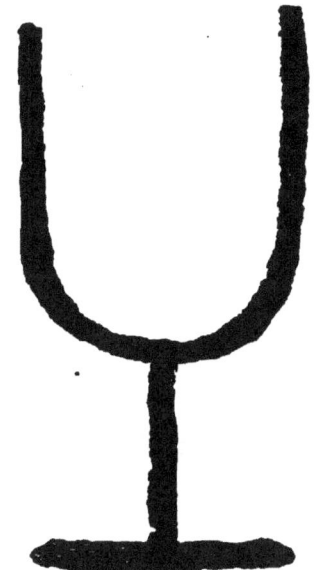

Mr. Guthrie and Miss E.
No contact.

No. 4. — Original Drawing.

No. 4. — Reproduction.

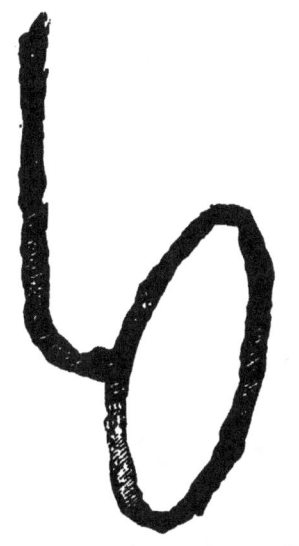

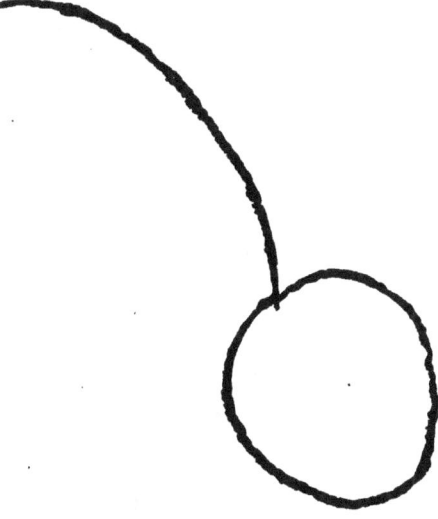

Mr. Guthrie and Miss E.
No contact.

No. 5.—Original Drawing.   No. 5.—Reproduction.

Mr. Guthrie and Miss E.
No contact.

No. 6.—Original Drawing.

Mr. Guthrie and Miss E.   No contact.

No. 6.—Reproduction.

Miss E. almost directly said, "Are you thinking of the bottom of the sea, with shells and fishes;" and then, "Is it a snail or a fish?"—then drew as above.

No. 7.—Original Drawing.

Mr. Gurney and Miss R.   Contact for half a minute before the reproduction was drawn.

No. 7.—Reproduction.

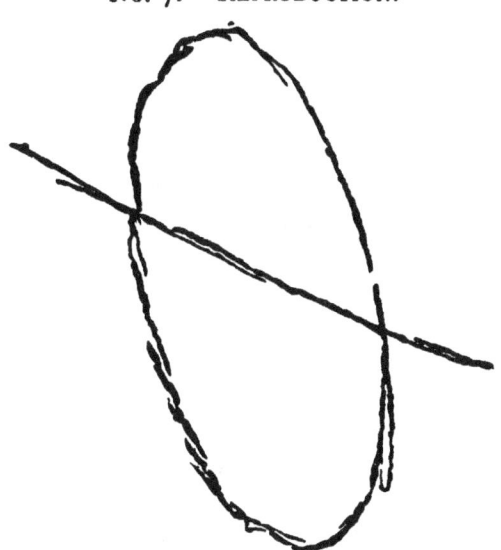

No. 8. — ORIGINAL DRAWING.   No. 8. — REPRODUCTION.

Mr. Gurney and Miss R.   No contact.

No. 9. — ORIGINAL DRAWING.

Mr. Birchall and Miss R.   No contact.

No. 9. — REPRODUCTION.

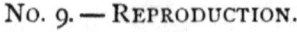
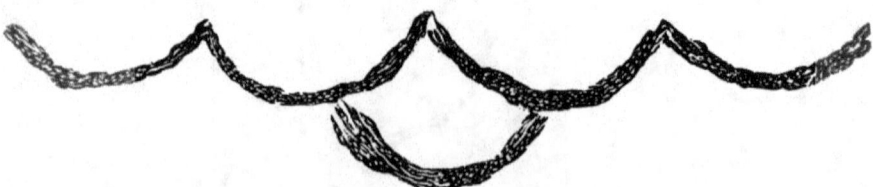

Miss R. said she seemed to see a lot of rings, as if they were moving, and
she could not get them steadily before her eyes.

No. 10.—Original Drawing.   No. 10.—Reproduction.

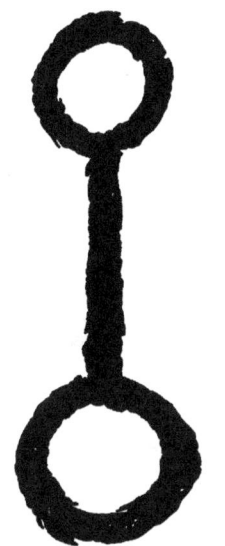 

Mr. Birchall and Miss R.   No contact.

No. 11.—Original Drawing.

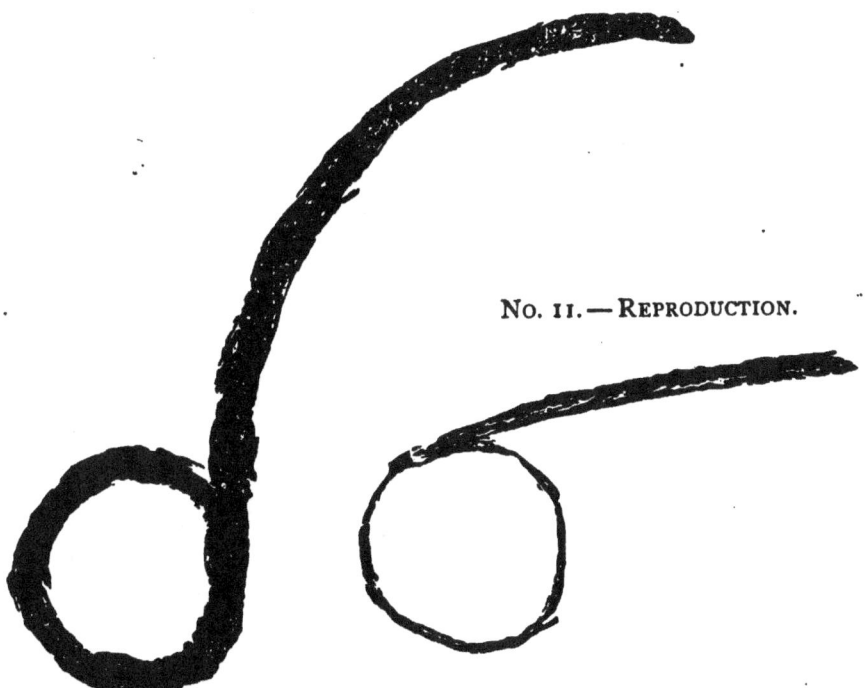

No. 11.—Reproduction.

Mr. Birchall and Miss E.   No contact.

NO. 12.—ORIGINAL DRAWING.

Mr. Steel and Miss R.   No contact.

NO. 12.—REPRODUCTION.

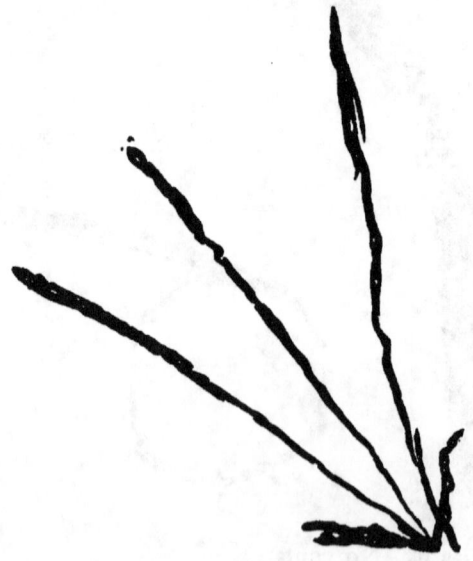

No. 13.—Original Drawing.   No. 13.—Reproduction.

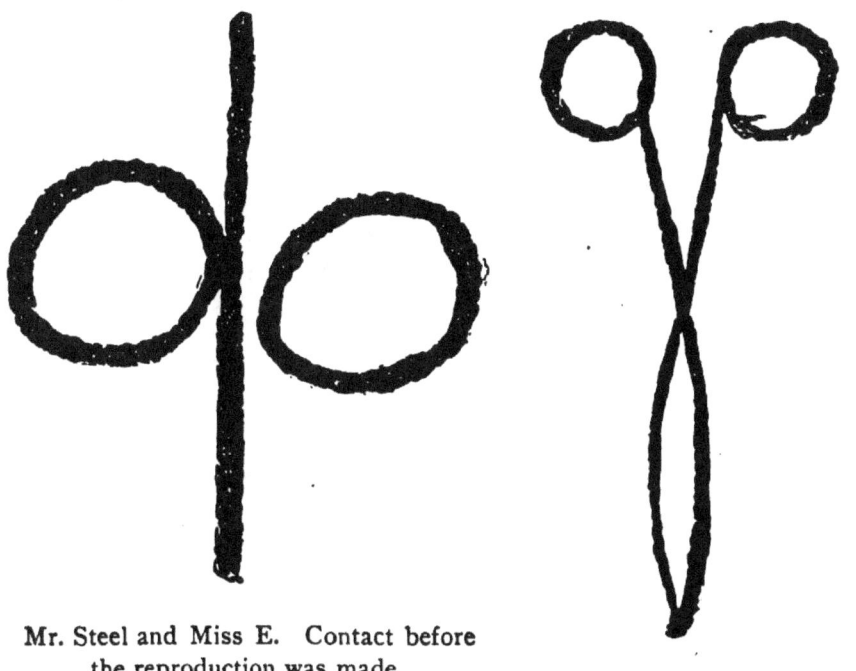

Mr. Steel and Miss E. Contact before
the reproduction was made.

No. 14.—Original Drawing.   No. 14.—Reproduction.

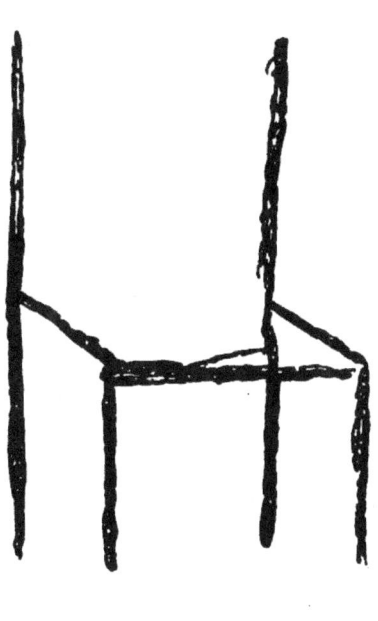

Mr. Hughes and Miss E. Contact
before the reproduction was made.

Miss E. said, " A box or chair badly
shaped,"—then drew as above.

No. 15.—Original Drawing.

Mr. Hughes and Miss E.   No contact.

No. 15.—Reproduction.

Miss E. said, "It is like a mask at a pantomime," and immediately drew as above.

No. 16. — Original Drawing.

Mr. Hughes and Miss E.   No contact.

No. 16. — Reproduction.

VI.

AT the meeting of the Society held Nov. 22, 1883, a fourth report was submitted by tne Committee on Thought-Transference as follows :

Since the last report was presented to the Society, the Committee on Thought-Transference have been steadily pursuing their inquiries, and have not only obtained a considerable amount of additional evidence confirmatory of their previous work, but also evidence of a new and important character. Moreover, we are happy to find that the inquiry is beginning to be pursued by independent groups of investigators throughout the country: some of these have communicated with us, and have courteously permitted us to examine their mode of experiment, and gladly availed themselves of the precautions upon which experience has taught us to insist. To Mr. Malcolm Guthrie, J.P., of Liverpool, we owe our warm thanks for his most capable and courteous co-operation, and we are glad to say that he has lately joined our Committee. Since his extensive series of experiments Mr. Guthrie has enlarged his range of experiments, and obtained remarkable success in the transference of visual impressions — diagrams and the like — of tastes, and of pains. The only sort of distinct sensation of which the transference yet remains to be obtained, is that of *smell*, — there being, of course, special difficulties in so arranging the experiment that a subject shall have no opportunity of detecting by direct means any strongly odorous substance which the agent is smelling close by. In many of Mr. Guthrie's later experiments the *sole* agent has been himself, or one or other of the gentlemen engaged with him in the investigation.

We trust that Mr. Guthrie's example will stimulate others among our members to conduct experiments of the same kind. Not all investigators, indeed, may have similar advantages of wide command of subjects for experiment; but any one among us may very possibly find in his own family circle some one subject of value; and it is, of course, in the family circle that it is easiest to secure that continual and patient repetition of experiments which seems essential to any marked success.

1. *Transference of Tastes.*

The experiments which we shall first detail have reference to the *transference of tastes.* This particular form of transferred sensation has been often experimented upon, by ourselves and by others, with subjects in the hypnotic state; but, so far as we know, Mr. Guthrie was the first person to procure the phenomenon when agent and percipient were both of them in a normal condition. There was no chance of collusion, conscious or unconscious; for the taste to be discerned was known to no one except the actual experimenters; and the sensations experienced were verbally described by the subjects (not written down), so that all danger of involuntary muscular guidance was eliminated.

The following series of experiments were made in Liverpool during the first week in September, 1883 : —

A selection of about twenty strongly-tasting substances was made. These substances were enclosed in small bottles and small parcels, precisely similar to one another, and kept carefully out of the range of vision of the subjects, who were, moreover, blindfolded, so that no grimaces made by the tasters could be seen. The subjects, in fact, had no means whatever of knowing, through the sense of sight, what was the substance tasted.

Smell had to be guarded against with still greater care. When the substance was odoriferous, the packet or bottle was opened outside the room, or at such a distance, and so cautiously, as to prevent any sensible smell from escaping. The experiments, moreover, were conducted in the close vicinity of a very large kitchen, whence a strong odor of beefsteak and onions proceeded during almost all the time occupied. The tasters took pains to keep their heads high above the subjects, and to avoid breathing with open mouth. One substance (coffee) tried was found to give off a slight smell, in spite of all precautions, and an experiment made with this has been omitted.

The tasters were Mr. Guthrie (M.G.), Mr. Gurney (E.G.), and Mr. Myers (M.). The percipients were two young ladies employed in Mr. Guthrie's establishment, whom we will call R. and E. The tasters lightly placed a hand on one of the shoulders or hands of the percipients. During the first experiments (September 3d and 4th) there were one or two other persons in the room, who, however, were equally ignorant as to the substance tasted. During the experiments silence was preserved. During the last fifteen experiments (September 5th) only M. G., E. G., and M., with the two percipients, were present. On this evening Miss E. was, unfortunately, suffering from sore throat, which seemed to blunt her susceptibility. On this occasion none of the substances were allowed even to enter the room where the percipients were. They were kept in a dark lobby outside, and taken by the investigators at random, so that often one investigator did not even know what the other took. Still less could any spy have discerned what was chosen, had such spy been there, which he certainly was *not*.

A very small portion of each substance used was found to be enough. The difficulty lies in keeping the mean between the *massive* impression of a large quantity of a salt, spice, bitter, or acid, which confounds the specific differences under each general head, and the *fading* impression which is apt to give merely a residual pungency, from which the characteristic flavor has escaped. It is necessary to allow some minutes to elapse between each experiment, as the imaginary taste seems to be fully as persistent as the real one.

September 3, 1883.

Expt.	Taster.	Percipient.	Substance.	Answers Given.
1...	M.	E. ...	Vinegar	" A sharp and nasty taste."
2...	M.	E. ...	Mustard........	" Mustard."
3...	M.	R. ...	Do.	" Ammonia."
4...	M.	E. ...	Sugar	" I still taste the hot taste of the the mustard."

September 4.

EXPT.	TASTER.	PERCIPIENT.	SUBSTANCE.	ANSWERS GIVEN.
5 ...	E. G. & M.	E. ..	Worcestershire sauce,	"Worcestershire sauce."
6 ...	M. G. ...	R. ..	Do.	"Vinegar."
7 ...	E. G. & M.	E. ..	Port wine	"Between eau de Cologne and beer."
8 ...	M. G. ...	R. ..	Do.	"Raspberry vinegar."
9 ...	E. G. & M.	E. ..	Bitter aloes	"Horrible and bitter."
10 ...	M. G. ...	R. ..	Alum	"A taste of ink — of iron — of vinegar. I feel it on my lips — it is as if I had been eating alum."
11 ...	M. G. ...	E. ...	Alum	(E. perceived that M. G. was *not* tasting bitter aloes, as E. G. and M. supposed, but something different. No distinct perception on account of the persistence of the bitter taste.)
12 ...	E. G. & M.	E. ..	Nutmeg	"Peppermint — no — what you put in puddings — nutmeg."
13 ...	M. G. ...	R. ...	Do.	"Nutmeg." [1]
14 ...	E. G. & M.	E. ..	Sugar	Nothing perceived.
15 ...	M. G. ...	R. ..	Do	Nothing perceived. (Sugar should be tried at an earlier stage in the series, as, after the aloes, we could scarcely taste it ourselves.)
16 ...	E. G. & M.	E. ...	Cayenne pepper ...	"Mustard."
17 ...	M. G. ...	R. ..	Do. ...	"Cayenne pepper." (After the cayenne we were unable to taste anything further that evening.)

September 5.

18 ...	E. G. & M.	E. ...	Carbonate of soda ..	Nothing perceived.

[1] In some cases *two* experiments were carried on simultaneously with the same substance; and when this was done, the first percipient was of course not told whether her answer was right or wrong. But it will perhaps be maintained that, when her answer was right, her agent unconsciously gave her an intimation of the fact by the pressure of his hand; and that she then coughed or made some audible signal to her companion, who followed suit. Whatever the theory may be worth, it will, we think, be seen that the success of the second percipient with the nutmeg was the only occasion, throughout the series, to which it can be applied.

September 5 (*continued*).

EXPT.	TASTER.	PERCIPIENT.	SUBSTANCE.	ANSWERS GIVEN.
19 ...	M. G. ...	R ...	Caraway seeds	"It feels like meal — like a seed loaf — caraway seeds." (The *substance* of the seeds seemed to be perceived before their *taste*.)
20 ...	E. G. & M.	E ...	Cloves	"Cloves."
21 ...	E. G. & M.	E ...	Citric acid.......	Nothing felt.
22 ...	M. G. ...	R ...	Do.	"Salt."
23 ...	E. G. & M.	E ...	Liquorice	"Cloves."
24 ...	M. G. ...	R ...	Cloves	"Cinnamon."
25 ...	E. G. & M.	E ...	Acid jujube	"Pear drop."
26 ...	M. G. ...	R ...	Do.	"Something hard, which is giving way; acid jujube."
27 ...	E. G. & M.	E ...	Candied ginger	"Something sweet and hot."
28 ...	M. G. ...	R ...	Do.	"Almond toffy." (M. G. took this ginger in the dark, and was some time before he realized that it was ginger.)
29 ...	E. G. & M.	E ...	Home-made Noyau..	"Salt."
30 ...	M. G. ...	R ...	Do. ..	"Port wine." (This was by far the most strongly smelling of the substances tried; the scent of kernels being hard to conceal. Yet it was named by E. as salt.)
31 ...	E. G. & M.	E ...	Bitter aloes	"Bitter."
32 ...	M. G. ...	R ...	Do.	Nothing felt.

We should have preferred in these experiments to use only substances which were wholly inodorous. But in order to get any description of tastes from the percipients it was necessary that the tastes should be either very decided or very familiar. It would be desirable, before entering on a series of experiments of this kind, to educate the palates of the percipients by accustoming them to a variety of chemical substances, and also by training them to distinguish, with shut eyes, between the more ordinary flavors. It is well known how much taste is helped by sight and determined by expectation; and when it is considered that the percipients in these cases were judging blindfold of the mere shadow of a savor, it will, perhaps, be thought that even some of their mistakes are not much wider of the mark than they might have been had a trace of the substance been actually placed upon their tongues.

The interest and novelty of the foregoing experiments consist in the fact, already mentioned, that the subjects were apparently in their normal waking state. It has long been on record that such transference of impressions may take place between a mesmeriser or hynoptist and a sensitive subject. But here no preliminary mesmeric passes nor fixation of the eyes had been resorted to; nor indeed have the subjects ever been mesmerized.

2. *Transference of Pains.*

The same subjects, Miss R. and Miss E., who proved sensitive to the transference of tastes, were also found sensitive to the transference of pains whilst in their normal waking state. Mr. Guthrie has made a number of experiments in this direction.

3. *Casual Experiments.*

We have received from correspondents in different parts of the country, records of more or less successful trials made among members of their own families. As a rule, however, these experiments have been too few and too fitful to be of much value; at the same time they are of interest as affording information that the faculty of thought-transference is probably tolerably widely diffused. Here, for example, is the result of a casual trial by one of our members, the Hon. Mrs. Fox Powys as percipient, with her husband as agent.

" I send the results of a trial my husband and I had alone. To me it seemed like magic ! We had tried, I think, three times before this, with indifferent success. I was the guesser, and he held my left hand with his right, and merely thought of a number. I sat with my eyes closed. The rapidity with which the thing was done astonished us ; the number seemed to flash instantaneously into my brain. In fact, so simultaneous was it

that I began to think that I, perhaps, had impressed the number
upon Colonel Powys' brain first. However, when we reversed
the operation, and my husband guessed, he was not at all successful. Here are our experiments; the complete series, including failures as well as successes, is given.

"First we tried single figures, and only one guess was
allowed.

NUMBER THOUGHT OF.	RESULT.
3	I perceived nothing.
2	I answered 2.
4	" 7.
6	I perceived nothing.
5	I answered 5.
9	" 9.
3	" 3.
8	" 8.

"Here, out of 8 trials, 5 were right. We now tried numbers
of two figures, and where a second guess was given it is
noted.

NUMBER THOUGHT OF.	RESULT.		
58	24		
36	36		
27	72	On a second guess, 27.	
69	28	"	" 82.
100	100		
42	42		
55	55		
22	79	"	" 97.
38	38		
30	42	"	" 78.
22	120	"	" 20.

"Here 5 were right the first time, and one the second time,
out of 11 trials. We tried again the next evening, but, out of
20, only got 5 right on the first trial, and 2 right on a second

trial. The secret of success the previous evening I believe to lie in the fact that I felt almost absolute confidence in my power to guess correctly, and to this height of confidence I have never since been able to attain."

The coincidences here recorded seem clearly beyond the power of pure chance to account for.

Another correspondent, writing from Brunswick Place, Leeds, sent to us an account of some successful experiments of his own, which, however, seemed probably due to mere muscular interpretation. We explained this to him, pointing out the precautions necessary to guard against the error. In reply, he writes to us as follows : —

"I have made a number of experiments since writing to you last ; perhaps the best of these was my finding a pin secreted in a purse which was in my sister's pocket. I also found the number of a bank note correctly, and correctly discovered 10 figures out of 12. But these experiments were made when contact was permitted, or by my running the agent's hand over a series of figures from o to 9. When I tried yesterday to tell the figures *without* contact, I failed completely.

"I then blindfolded my sister, aged thirteen, and placed a piece of pencil and paper before her. Then I drew, with a piece of chalk on a school-slate, a simple diagram (a circle with a cross inside), without her hearing the scratching of the chalk. To my surprise she drew the enclosed, in about a minute, there being no contact between us, and I giving no indication whatever, merely thinking and staring at the slate. I then made other experiments in a similar way, and enclose you the results."

These, and a few other diagrams subsequently received, made in all ten trials, with diagrams of various random and irregular shapes. Of the ten trials six were as good reproductions of the original as could have been drawn had the child seen the original drawing and attempted to draw it blindfolded. The remaining four bore less, but still some, resemblance to the original. The honorary secretary of the committee has visited this correspondent in Leeds, and seen the way in which the experiments were made.   As far as could be judged from such a visit, no information could have reached the percipient through the ordinary channels of sense.   The agent is a highly intelligent young man, and quite alive to the precautions necessary to be taken to avoid obvious errors of experiment.

The following diagrams are part of the series referred to. Professor Barrett has seen the agent, Mr. J. W. Smith, of Brunswick Place, Leeds, and his sister, the percipient, and has carefully explained to them the necessary precautions; but their description of the mode in which they had worked before this interview convinced him that those previous trials had been conducted with due care, and that the results were genuine. The experiments have been made throughout without contact. The first four of the diagrams here engraved were made before Professor Barrett's visit; the last four have been made since his visit.

ORIGINAL DRAWING.

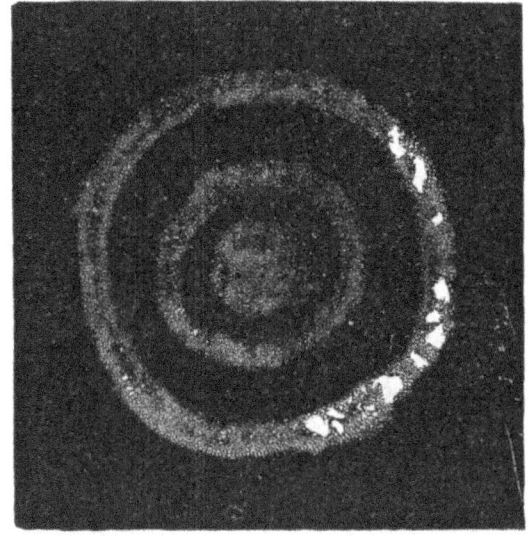

REPRODUCTION.

ORIGINAL DRAWING.

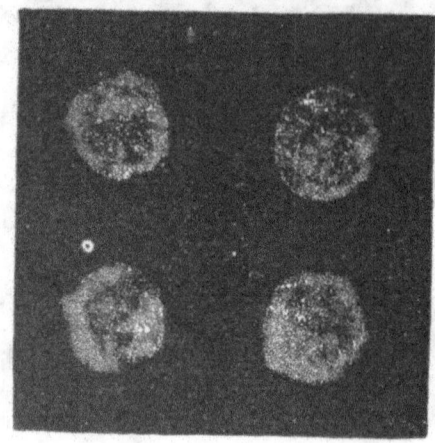

REPRODUCTION.

ORIGINAL DRAWING.

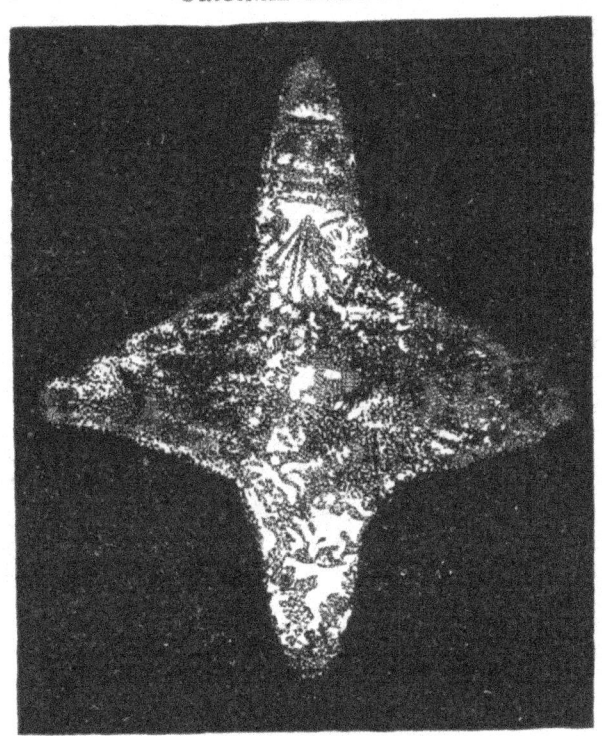

REPRODUCTION.

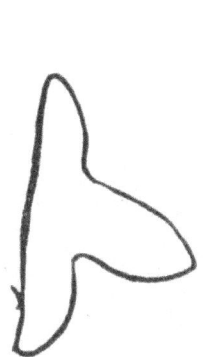
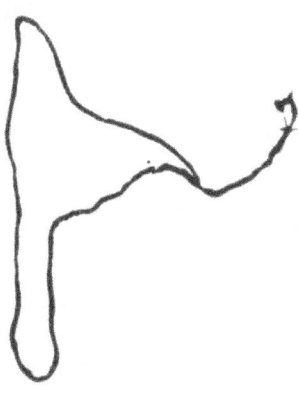

ORIGINAL DRAWING.

REPRODUCTION.

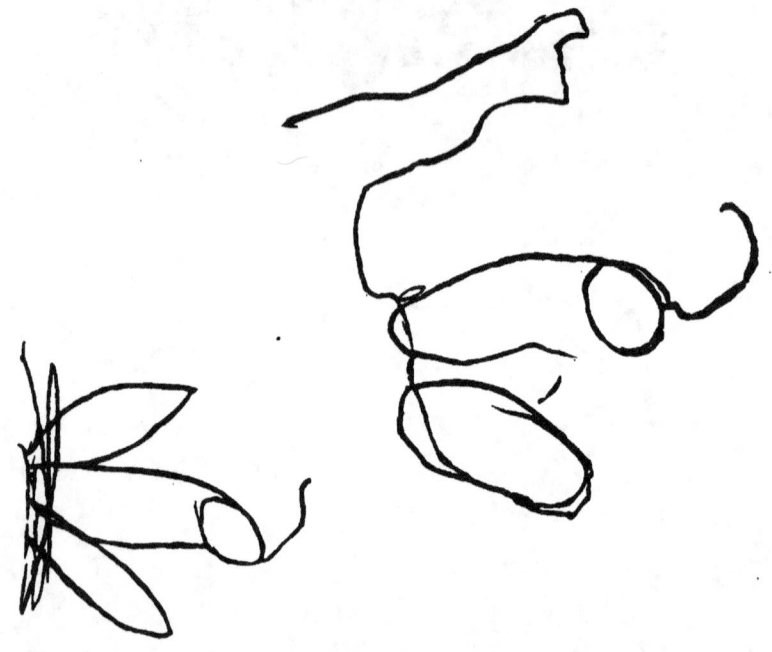

ORIGINAL DRAWING.

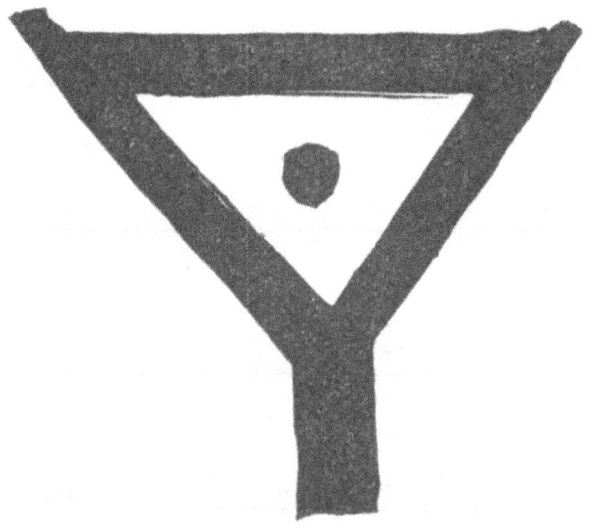

REPRODUCTION.

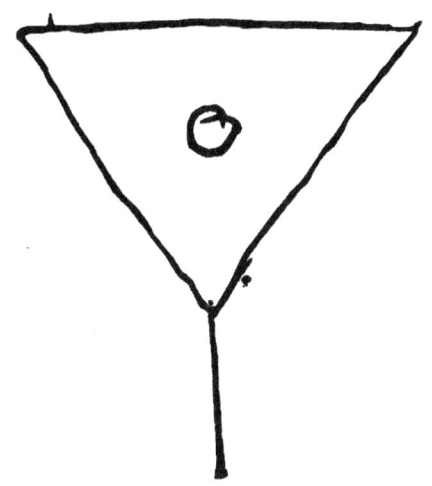

ORIGINAL DRAWING.

REPRODUCTION.

ORIGINAL DRAWING.

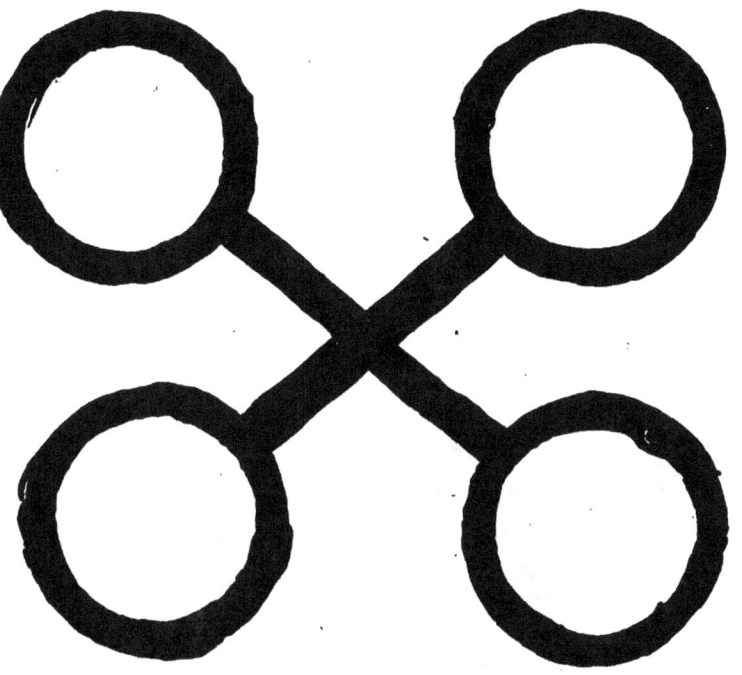

REPRODUCTION.

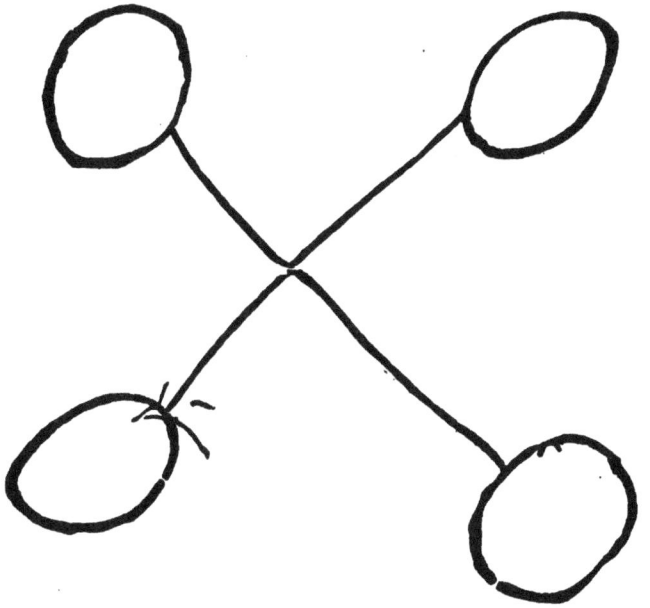

ORIGINAL DRAWING.

REPRODUCTION.

The closing portion of the fourth report on Thought-Transference follows : —

The following is an extract from a letter written to one of us by Mr. R. Gibson, of Limerick. He has since supplied us with additional details, and tells us that the subject (who has a large apothecary's business), and several of the agents, had previously been quite incredulous as to the phenomenon.

March 20, 1884. — On last Tuesday week we were trying some experiments at a friend's house, and a Mr. Day, who was there, told the number thought of in five different cases by five different people, — told them one after the other without a bungle or any hesitation whatever. After these five consecutive trials he got a violent headache, and on trying again could not tell any more. He was successful by picturing to himself (with his eyes shut) a blackboard, and the number seemed at once to stand out on it in white.

The headache is an interesting, but (we are happy to say) not a frequent feature of these experiments. The imagining of the blackboard is a device worth noting.

The following account was received, some weeks ago, from Miss Crabbe (Gordon College, Chatham Street, Liverpool), a lady known to two members of the committee : —

One evening, at a rectory where I have been staying, we were trying pin-finding, when I said I had seen much more wonderful things than that done, and told them of what is done in your Society, such as placing figures and other objects behind people, etc.

They were *very* sceptical about it, — said it could *not* be done without trickery, collusion, etc.; that it was nonsense, etc.; and we had quite a lively argument about it, for I stuck to my point, and vowed it could be and *was* done. At last the rector said he would try it, for that if any one could do it he could. He acted as agent, and his daughter as percipient. The latter was blindfolded and placed in the usual position; the background was a large piece of white cardboard, and on that I pinned a pink oblong card, and, to my astonishment, in about a minute or two's time Miss —— described it; for I must confess I

expected a failure on account of the scepticism of all parties.

Of course this success slightly changed their opinion, and
they tried again. The next object I placed up was a round fan
or hand-screen, which was most accurately described; the order
we proceeded in was first, color; second, shape; and third, object.
Object after object was tried, and *every* time was a success.
They declared it was wonderful. Night after night we tried it,
and the whole time I was there Miss —— never once made the
slightest error, and often named the object after the lapse of a
second or so, with no second guess.

We tried everything we could think of, including spoons,
door-keys, oranges. In describing the latter, Miss —— said:
"It is something with a reddish tinge, not quite round, but a
little flat at the top and bottom. Oh, I see; it is an orange."

After the objects, we tried taste-transference. The effect was
marvellous. Salt, sugar, nutmeg, etc., were tasted by Mr. ——
and transferred to his daughter.

Next we tried the number-reading, which was also a grand
success; in this case we *sometimes* reversed the agent and percipient, Mr. —— acting as the latter (and not as the former, as
on the previous occasions), and either Miss —— or I as the
agent. Whichever plan we took proved successful, and we tried
very many times. The percipient wrote the numbers down
while the agent was in contact with either the left hand or the
forehead.

After the number-writing, we tried objects again, *without*
contact. This was also done without an error, Mr. —— acting
as agent, and making a few downward passes while fixing his
mind on the object to be described.

Next we tried reading sentences written on the background;
i. e., I wrote in large hand on a card, "Don't kill dogs;"
then, "Thou shalt not kill," both of which were read by Miss
——, with the exception of one word, where I stopped her on
account of an interruption. Then Mr. —— acted as percipient
and Miss —— as agent, and I wrote up, "Be quick." Mr. ——
said, "B-e — be, q-u-i-e-t—quiet." "No," we said, "not quite

right." "No," he said, "the last two letters are c-k, not e-t; it is 'Be quick.'" Miss ——, however, never even made that much of a failure.

Of all the experiments I have seen performed, I *never* saw any to equal these, which were all so quickly and accurately made. I can tell you I felt elated at having turned sceptics into such clever performers.

In a second letter Miss Crabbe adds : —

When I proposed trying taste-transference, I said to Mr. —— : "It must be something that has no smell," whereupon he replied, " Well, write down the name of anything you wish me to taste on a piece of paper." I did so, writing the word "ginger." He then put the paper in *his mouth*, and I suppose imagined he tasted the ginger, for in a minute or two Miss —— said what it was. The reason I did not mention this before is that I am not sure whether Miss —— actually *tasted* the ginger, or whether the *word* was impressed on her mind, and she felt bound to say it. This was the first experiment in taste-transference ; afterwards I always gave the substance to Mr. —— to taste himself first, and then his daughter evidently did really perceive the taste.

In the *sentence-reading* I wrote up *first*, " Don't kill dogs," but some one entered the room before this was read at all, and an interruption ensued, whereupon I said, " Never mind that one now, don't tell us anything about it, and I will write another." I then wrote, " Thou shalt not kill." This was read correctly, and immediately afterwards Miss —— said, " I may as well tell you what I thought the first sentence was. Was it — Don't kill ? " and then she made some remark about the last word being a short one, or something of the kind, but I really don't remember what the remark was.

4. *Unconscious Muscular Action.*

The subject of thought-reading is just now in a rather singular position ; for it is obtaining immense vogue throughout the country by dint of public exhibitions which, however clever and interesting, have no claim to be considered thought-reading at all. These exhibitions usually produce a perfect deluge of letters in the local journals, in which the "willing game" and its results are discussed from every possible standpoint and in every possible key, by believers, disbelievers, and doubters. In the more scientific contributions to this correspondence, expression is usually given to three distinct views, each of which deserves serious attention.

Some contributors are certain to give an adequate explanation of the process of "muscle-reading"—an explanation which easily covers the successes of the public performers, as well as ninety-nine out of one hundred cases of success in the "willing game."

Some one else is pretty sure to put forward the hypothesis strongly suggested by the one hundredth case of the "willing game"—where what is done is of so subtle or complicated a kind as to raise doubts whether unconscious muscular pressure, or rather *release* of pressure, in a certain direction, is adequate to account for it; and one is tempted to look deeper for the springs of action, and to conceive the governance of one organism by another through some sort of nervous induction.

And finally, some prudent correspondent will point out that— as long as the form of experiments adopted is the performance of some *action*—the problem can never be solved as long as *contact* of any sort is allowed between the "willer" and the "willed"; and will perhaps do us the honor to refer to some of our own experiments, in which success in far more delicate operations than pin-finding and number-writing has been attained without contact.

It is clearly only to experiments performed under this last condition—a condition which precludes any unconscious guidance from the agent — that the word "thought-reading" can be safely applied. That name, of course, in no way implies the absence of a physical basis for the phenomena; the theory of brain-waves (which would be only an instance of "nervous induction") has been suggested to supply such a basis. But of such a *physical basis* we know nothing; of the *psychical facts* we know a great deal, all of them being, in various forms, transfer-

ences of impression or idea from mind to mind otherwise than
by the recognized sensory channels. The difference between these
cases and the public exhibitions of muscular and tactile sensibility is of course fundamental ; and it is unfortunate that
the word "thought-reading" should have become associated
with the latter. Even for the genuine cases "*thought-transference*" is a much better expression; the other term having
apparently conveyed to some persons the notion that, if once
the reality of the phenomena were established, we should all be
able to read each other's secrets.

We must emphatically repeat, then, what we laid down in our
first report,— that wherever contact is permitted, success in the
performance of a desired *action* must be attributed to indications given by the " willer " — that his unconscious and involuntary variations in pressure are unconsciously and involuntarily, or
consciously and voluntarily, interpreted by the percipient.[1] We
have thought it desirable to make a series of experiments to
ascertain what can be done in this way; and the results have
been most striking, but not unexpected. One of our members
has given a lecture on muscle-reading in the Ulster Hall, Bel-
fast, where he performed the following muscular feat, as described by a local newspaper. "A £5 note was handed to
Mr. W. Gray, who fixed the number of it in his mind, the
lecturer being blindfolded. The blackboard was brought into
requisition, having five sections or colors marked upon it. Mr.
Sugden, whose right hand, holding a piece of chalk, was in
contact with Mr. Gray's left, then made the figures 5, 5, 3, 4, 0
with great deliberation, and these were acknowledged as the
correct number of the bank-note." Further experiments have
been made by the honorary secretary of the committee with another subject. Numbers thought of have been written with per-

---

[1] The same objection naturally applies to all cases where the subject *writes
down* something which is in the agent's mind — the *action*, due to unconscious
guidance, being then the movements of the pencil or chalk. The objection
does not apply to cases where the subject gives his notion of the "transferred impression "— word, number, taste, or whatever it may be — *by word
of mouth.*

fect accuracy by the subject, when the tips of the agent's fingers were allowed to rest on the hand that held the pencil, *provided* that the agent himself followed the movements of the pencil with his eye. When the agent's eyes were averted, and there was no more chance of unconscious guidance, failure was at once the result. Diagrams have been accurately reproduced in like manner, while failure has inevitably followed the closing or blindfolding of the agent's eyes. With a lady as agent, two drawings were even reproduced with a considerable degree of accuracy when her fingers lightly touched the subject's left hand, he holding the pencil in his right.

We may conclude with a practical suggestion. Public perform-ances, such as those which are exciting so much interest through-out the country, have this advantage — that they invariably set people to work in private houses : and it would clearly be a great thing if this result could be made useful as well as amusing. We would venture, then, to suggest to those who feel drawn to the pursuit, that, instead of repeating the old " willing game," and merely re-proving what has been proved a hundred times before, they should devote themselves to experiments *without contact*, or else adopt some form of experiment where the subject has only to *name* an object or sensation — and so aid in the establishment of facts completely new to science. Cards, numbers, names, diagrams, all supply good forms of experiment.

VII.

AT the meeting of the Society, held March 28, 1884, Professor Oliver J. Lodge, Professor of Physics in University College, Liverpool, presented a paper entitled, " Some Experiments in Thought-Transference," as follows : —

Members of the Society for Psychical Research are all perfectly aware of the experiments in thought-transference which have been originated and carried out by Mr. Malcolm Guthrie, in Liverpool.

Perhaps it may not be considered impertinent, since it bears on the question of responsibility and genuineness, if I state that Mr. Guthrie holds an important position in Liverpool, being a Justice of the Peace, and an active member of the governing bodies of several public institutions, among others of the new University College ; that he is a severe student of philosophy, and the author of several works bearing on the particular doctrines of Mr. Herbert Spencer. I may also say that he is a relative of Professor Frederick Guthrie, and that he has exhibited in this experimental research such care and systematic vigilance as might perhaps have been expected on Mr. Francis Galton's principles, and such as would, if properly directed, have placed him in a high rank of experimental philosophers. I may also remind you of what he himself has here said, viz., that he is a partner in the chief drapery establishment in Liverpool, and that it is among the employees of that large business that the two percipients hereafter referred to were accidentally discovered.

Let it be understood that the experiments are Mr. Guthrie's, and that my connection with them is simply this, — that after Mr. Guthrie had laboriously carried out a long series of experiments and had published many of his results, he set about endeavoring to convince such students of science as he could lay his hands upon in Liverpool; and with this object he appealed to me, among others, to come and witness, and within limits modify, the experiments in such a way as would satisfy me of their genuineness and perfect good faith.

Yielding to his entreaty, I consented, and have been, I suppose, at some dozen sittings; at first simply looking on so as to grasp the phenomena, but afterwards taking charge of the experiments — Mr. Guthrie himself often not being present, though he was always within call in another room, ready to give advice and assistance when desired.

In this way I had every opportunity of examining and varying the minute conditions of the phenomena so as to satisfy myself of their genuine and objective character, in the same way as one is accustomed to satisfy one's self as to the truth and genuineness of any ordinary physical fact.

I did not feel at liberty to modify the experiments very largely, — in other words to try essentially new ones, — because that would have been interfering with Mr. Guthrie's prerogative. I only regarded it as my business to satisfy myself as to the genuineness and authenticity of the phenomena already described by Mr. Guthrie. If I had merely witnessed facts as a passive spectator I should most certainly not publicly report upon them. So long as one is bound to accept imposed conditions and merely witness what goes on, I have no confidence in my own penetration, and am perfectly sure that a conjurer could impose on me, possibly even to the extent of making me think that he was not imposing on me; but when one has the control of the circumstances, can change them at will, and arrange one's own experiments, one gradually acquires a belief in the phenomena observed quite comparable to that induced by the repetition of ordinary physical experiments.

It is only on these grounds that I have been asked to report progress to-night, and it is only on these grounds that I have consented.

After this long preamble you may be disappointed to hear that I have no striking or new phenomenon to report, but only a few more experiments in the simplest and most elementary form of what is called Thought-transference; though certainly what I have to describe falls under the head of "thought-transference" proper, and is not explicable by the merely mechanical transfer of impressions, exhibited before large audiences, signalized by sensational articles in the daily press, and more properly described as muscle-reading.

In using the term "thought-transference" I would ask to be understood as doing so for convenience, because the observed facts can conveniently be grouped under such a title; but I would not be understood as implying that I hold any theory on the subject. It is a most dangerous thing to attempt to convey a theory by a phrase, and, probably, if I held any theory on the subject, I should be more guarded in my language, and should require many words to set it fotth. As it is, the phrase describes correctly enough what appears to take place, viz., that one person may, under favorable conditions, receive a faint impression of a thing which is strongly present in the mind, or thought, or sight, or sensorium of another person not in contact, and may be able to describe or draw it more or less correctly. But how the transfer takes place, or whether there is any transfer at all, or what is the physical reality underlying the terms "mind," "consciousness," "impression," and the like, and whether this thing we call "mind" is located in the person, or in the space round him, or in both, or neither; whether indeed the term "location," as applied to mind, is utter nonsense and simply meaningless, — concerning all these things I am absolutely blank, and have no hypothesis whatsoever. I may, however, be permitted to suggest a rough and crude analogy. That the brain is the organ of consciousness is patent, but that consciousness is located in the brain is what no psychologist ought to assert; for just as the energy of an electric charge, though apparently on the conductor, is not on the conductor, but in all the space round it; just as the energy of an electric current, though apparently in the copper wire, is certainly not all in the copper wire and possibly not any of it; so it may be that the sensory consciousness of a person, though apparently located in his brain, may be conceived of as also existing like a faint echo in space, or in other brains, though these are ordinarily too busy and pre-occupied to notice it.

The experiments which I have witnessed proceed in this sort of way. One person is told to keep in a perfectly passive condition, with a mind as vacant as possible; and to assist this condition the organs of sense are unexcited, the eyes being bandaged and silence maintained. It might be as well to shut out even the ordinary street hum by plugging the ears, but as a matter of fact this was not done.

A person thus kept passive is the "percipient." In the experiments I witnessed, the percipient was a young lady, one or other of two who had been accidentally found to possess the necessary power. Whether it is a common power or not I do not know. So far as I am aware very few persons have been tried. I myself tried, but failed abjectly. It was easy enough to picture things to one's self, but they did not appear to be impressed on me from without, nor did any of them bear the least resemblance to the object in the agent's mind. [For instance, I said a pair of scissors instead of the five of diamonds, and things like that.] Nevertheless, the person acting as percipient is in a perfectly ordinary condition, and can in no sense be said to be in a hypnotic state, unless this term be extended to include the emptiness of mind produced by blindfolding and silence. To all appearance a person in a brown study is far more hypnotized than the percipients I saw, who usually unbandaged their own eyes and chatted between successive experiments.

Another person sitting near the percipient, sometimes at first holding her hands, but usually and ordinarily without any contact at all, but with a distinct intervening distance, was told to think hard of a particular object, either a name, or a scene, or a thing, or of an object or drawing set up in a good light and in a convenient position for staring at. This person is the "agent," and has, on the whole, the hardest time of it. It is a most tiring and tiresome thing to stare at a letter, or a triangle, or a donkey, or a teaspoon, and to think of nothing else for the space of two or three minutes. Whether the term "thinking" can properly be applied to such barbarous concentration of mind as this I am not sure; but I can answer for it that if *difficulty* is an important element in the definition of "thinking," then it is difficult enough in all conscience.

Very frequently more than one agent is employed, and when two or three people are in the room they are all told to think of the object more or less strenuously; the idea being that wandering thoughts in the neighborhood certainly cannot help, and may possibly hinder, the clear transfer of impression. As regards the question whether, when several agents are thinking, only one is doing the work, or whether all really produce some effect, I have made a special experiment, which leads me to conclude that more than one agent can be active at the same time. We conjecture that several agents are probably more powerful than one, but that a confusedness of impression may sometimes be produced by different agents attending to different parts or aspects of the object : this, however, is mere conjecture.

Most people seem able to act as agents, though some appear to do better than others. I can hardly say whether I am much good at it or not. I have not often tried alone, and in the majority of cases when I have tried I have failed; on the other hand, I have once or twice apparently succeeded. We have many times succeeded with agents quite disconnected from the percipients in ordinary life, and sometimes complete strangers to them. Mr. Birchall, the head master of the Birkdale Industrial School, frequently acted; and the house physician at the Eye and Ear Hospital, Dr. Shears, had a successful experiment, acting alone, on his first and only visit. All suspicion of a pre-arranged code is thus rendered impossible, even to outsiders who are unable to witness the obvious fairness of all the experiments.

The object looked at by the agent is placed usually on a small, black, opaque, wooden screen between the percipient and agents, but sometimes it is put on a larger screen behind the percipient. The objects were kept in an adjoining room, and were selected and brought in by me, with all due precaution, after the percipient was blindfolded. I should say, however, that no reliance was placed on, or care taken in, the bandaging. It was merely done because the percipient preferred it to merely shutting the eyes. After recent experiments on blindfolding by members of the Society, I certainly would not rely on any form of bandaging; the opacity of the wooden screen on which the object was placed was the thing really depended on, and it was noticed that no mirrors or indistinct reflectors were present. The only surface at all suspicious was the polished top of the small table on which the opaque screen usually stood. But as the screen sloped backwards at a slight angle, it was impossible for the object on it to be thus mirrored. Moreover, sometimes I covered the table with paper, and very often it was not used at all, but the object was placed on a screen or a settee behind the percipient; and one very striking success was obtained with the object placed on a large drawing-board, loosely swathed in a black silk college gown, and with the percipient immediately behind the said drawing-board, and almost hidden by it.

As regards collusion and trickery, every one who has witnessed the absolutely genuine and artless manner in which the impressions are described, has been perfectly convinced of the transparent honesty of purpose of all concerned. This, however, is not evidence to persons who have not been present, and to them I can only say that to the best of my scientific belief no collusion or trickery was possible under the varied circumstances of the experiments.

A very interesting question presents itself as to *what* is really transmitted, whether it is the idea or name of the object, or whether it is the visual impression. To examine this I frequently drew things without any name — perfectly irregular drawings. I am bound to say that these irregular and unnameable productions have always been rather difficult, though they have at times been imitated fairly well; but it is not at all strange that a faint impression of an unknown object should be harder to grasp and reproduce than a faint impression of a familiar one, — such as a letter, a common name, a teapot, or a pair of scissors. Moreover, in some very interesting cases the idea or name of the object was certainly the thing transferred, and not the visual impression at all; this specially happened with one of the two percipients; and, therefore, probably in every case, the fact of the object having a name would assist any faint impression of its appearance which might be received.

As to *aspect*, *i. e.*, inversion or perversion, so far as my experience goes, it seems perfectly accidental whether the object will be drawn by the percipient in its actual position, or in the inverted or perverted position. This is very curious, if true, and would certainly not have been expected by me. Horizontal objects are never described as vertical, nor *vice versâ;* and slanting objects are usually drawn with the right amount of slant.

In proceeding to the details of the actual experiments, it would take far too long to recount the whole — failures as well as successes. I shall only describe a few, from which a more or less obvious moral may be drawn.

The two percipients are Miss R. and Miss E. Miss R. is the more prosaic, staid, and self-contained personage, and she it is who gets the best quasi-visual impression, but she is a bad drawer, and does not reproduce it very well.

Miss E. is, I should judge, of a more sensitive temperament, seldom being able to preserve a strict silence, for instance, and she it is who more frequently jumps to the idea or name of the object without being able so frequently to see it.

I was anxious to try both percipients at once, so as to compare their impressions, but I have not met with much success under these conditions, and usually, therefore, have had to try one at a time — the other being frequently absent or in another room, though also frequently present and acting as part or sole agent.

I once tried a double agent — that is, not two agents thinking of the same thing, but two agents each thinking of a different thing. A mixed and curiously double impression was thus produced and described by the percipient, and both the objects were correctly drawn.

DESCRIPTION OF SOME OF THE EXPERIMENTS.

In order to describe the experiments briefly I will put in parentheses everything said by me or by the agent, and in quotation marks all the remarks of the percipient. The first seven experiments are all that were made on one evening with the particular percipient, and they were rapidly performed.

A. *Experiments with Miss R. as Percipient.*

First Agent, Mr. Birchall, holding hands. No one else present except myself.

Object — a blue square of silk. — (Now, it's going to be a color; ready.) "Is it green?" (No.) "It's something between green and blue — peacock." (What shape?) She drew a rhombus.

[N. B. — It is not intended to imply that this was a success by any means, and it is to be understood that it was only to make a start on the first experiment that so much help was given as is involved in saying "it's a color." When they are simply told "it's an object," or, what is much the same, when nothing is said at all, the field for guessing is practically infinite. When no remark at starting is recorded none was made, except such an one as "Now we are ready," by myself.]

Next object — a key on a black ground. — (It's an object.) In a few seconds she said, "It's bright — it looks like a key." Told to draw it she drew it just inverted.

Next object — three gold studs in morocco case. — "Is it yellow? Something gold — something round — a locket or a watch, perhaps." (Do you see more than one round?) "Yes, there seem to be more than one. Are there three rounds? — three rings." (What do they seem to be set in?) "Something bright like beads." [Evidently not understanding or attending to the question.] Told to unblindfold herself and draw, she drew the three rounds in a row quite correctly, and then sketched round them absently the outline of the case; which seemed, therefore, to have been apparent to her, though she had not consciously attended to it. It was an interesting and striking experiment.

Next object — a pair of scissors standing partly open with their points down. — "Is it a bright object? — Something long ways [indicating verticality] — a pair of scissors standing up — a little bit open." Time, about a minute altogether. She then drew her impression, and it was correct in every particular. The object in this experiment was on a settee behind her, but its position had to be pointed out to her when, after the experiment, she wanted to see it.

Next object — a drawing of a right-angled triangle on its side. — (It 's a drawing.) She drew an isosceles triangle on its side.

Next — a circle with a chord across it. — She drew two detached ovals, one with a cutting line across it.

Next — a drawing of a Union Jack pattern. — As usual in drawing experiments, Miss R. remained silent for perhaps a

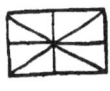

ORIGINAL.

REPRODUCTION.

minute; then she said, "Now I am ready." I hid the object; she took off the handkerchief, and proceeded to draw on paper placed ready in front of her. She this time drew all the lines of the figure except the horizontal middle one. She was obviously much tempted to draw this, and, indeed, began it two or three times faintly, but ultimately said, "No, I 'm not sure," and stopped.

I will now describe an experiment indicating that one agent may be better than another.

Object — the three of hearts. — Miss E. and Mr. Birchall both present as agents, but Mr. Birchall holding percipient's hands at first. "Is it a black cross — a white ground with a black cross on it?" Mr. Birchall now let Miss E. hold hands instead of himself, and Miss R. very soon said, "Is it a card?" (Right.) "Are there three spots on it? Don't know what they are. I don't think I can get the color. They are one above the other, but they seem three round spots. I think they 're red, but am not clear."

Next object — a playing card with a blue anchor painted on it slantwise instead of pips. — No contact at all this time, but another lady, Miss R——d, who had entered the room, assisted Mr. B. and Miss E. as agents. "Is it an anchor — a little on the slant." (Do you see any color?) "Color is black. It's a nicely drawn anchor." When asked to draw, she sketched part of it, but had evidently half forgotten it, and, not knowing the use of the cross arm, she could only indicate that there was something more there, but she couldn't remember what. Her drawing had the right slant exactly.

Another object — two pair of coarse lines crossing; drawn in red chalk, and set up at some distance from agents. No contact. "I only see lines crossing." She saw no color. She afterwards drew them quite correctly, but very small.

Double object. — It was now that I arranged the double object between Miss R——d and Miss E., who happened to be sitting nearly facing one another. The drawing was a square on one side of the paper, a cross on the other. Miss R——d looked at

ORIGINAL.   REPRODUCTION.

the side with the square on it. Miss E. looked at the side with the cross. Neither knew what the other was looking at — nor did the percipient know that anything unusual was being tried. Mr. Birchall was silently asked to take off his attention, and he got up and looked out of window before the drawings were brought in, and during the experiment. There was no contact. Very soon Miss R. said, "I see things moving about — I seem to see two things — I see first one up there and then one down there — I don't know which to draw — I can't see either distinctly." (Well, anyhow, draw what you have seen.) She took off the bandage and drew first a square, and then said, "Then there was the other thing as well — afterwards they seemed to go into one," and she drew a cross inside the square, from corner to corner, adding afterwards, "I don't know what made me put it inside."

The next is a case of a perfect stranger acting as agent by

himself at the first trial. Dr. Shears, house physician at the Eye and Ear Infirmary, came down to see the phenomena, and Miss R. having arrived before the others, Mr. Guthrie proposed his trying as agent alone. Dr. Shears, therefore, held Miss R.'s hand while I set up in front of him a card: nothing whatever being said as to the nature of the object..

Object — the five of clubs, at first on a white ground. " Is it something bright?" (No answer, but I changed the object to a black ground where it was more conspicuous.) "A lot of black with a white square on it." (Go on.) " Is it a card?" (Yes.) "Are there five spots on it?" (Yes.) " Black ones." (Right.) " I can't see the suit, but I think it's spades."

Another object at same sitting, but with several agents, no contact, a drawing of this form —

ORIGINAL.

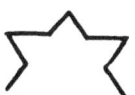
REPRODUCTION.

" I can see something, but I am sure I can't draw it, — it's something with points all round it, — it's a star, — or like a triangle within a triangle." Asked to draw it, she expressed reluctance, said it was too difficult, and drew part of a star figure, evidently a crude reproduction of the original, but incomplete. She then began afresh by drawing a triangle, but was unable to proceed.

I then showed her the object for a few seconds. She exclaimed, "Oh yes, that's what I saw. — I understand it now." I said, "Well, now draw it." She made a more complete attempt, but it was no more really like the original than the first had been.

Experiments at a Sitting in the room of Dr. Herdman, Professor of Zoology at University College.

Object — a drawing of the outline of a flag. — Miss R. as per-

ORIGINAL.   REPRODUCTION.

cipient in contact with Miss E. as agent. Very quickly Miss R. said, "It's a little flag," and when asked to draw, she drew it fairly well, but perverted. I showed her the flag (as usual after a success), and then took it away to the drawing-place to fetch something else. I made another drawing, but, instead of bring- ing it, I brought the flag back again and set it up in the same place as before, but inverted. There was no contact this time. Miss R——d and Miss E. were acting as agents.

Object — same flag inverted. — After some time, Miss R. said, " No, I can't see anything this time. I still see that flag — The flag keeps bothering me — I shan't do it this time." Presently I said, " Well, draw what you saw, anyway." She said, " I only saw the same flag, but perhaps it had a cross on it." So she drew a flag in the same position as before, but added a cross to it. Questioned as to aspect, she said, " Yes, it was just the same as before."

Object — an oval gold locket, hanging by a bit of string, with a little price label attached. — Placed like the former object on a large drawing-board, swathed in a college gown. The percipient, Miss R., close behind the said board and almost hidden by it. Agents, Miss R——d and Miss E., sitting in front; no contact; nothing said. " I see something gold — something hanging — like a gold locket." (What shape ?) " It 's oval," indicat-

ing with her fingers correctly. (Very good so far, tell us something more) — meaning ticket at top. No more said. When
shown the object, she said, " Oh yes, it was just like that," but
she had seen nothing of the little paper ticket.

*Next object — a watch and chain pinned up to the board as on a
waistcoat.* — This experiment was a failure, and is only interesting because the watch-ticking sounded abnormally loud, sufficient to give any amount of hint to a person on the lookout for
such sense indications. But it is very evident to those witnessing
the experiments that the percipient is in a quite different attitude
of mind to that of the clever guesser, and ordinary sense indications seem wholly neglected. I scarcely expected, however, that
the watch-ticking could pass unnoticed, though indeed we shuf-
fled our feet to drown it somewhat, but so it was ; and all we
got was " something bright, either steel or silver — Is it anything like a pair of scissors ? " (Not a bit.)

I have now done with the selection of experiments in which
Miss R. acted as percipient ; and I will describe some of those
made with Miss E. As a rule, these seemed perhaps less satisfactory and complete at the time, but there are several points of
considerable interest noticeable in connection with them.

B. — Experiments with Miss E. as Percipient.

Object — an oblong piece of red (cerise) silk. — Agent, Mr. B., in
contact. " Red." (What sort of red ?) " A dark red." (What
shape ?) " One patch." (Well, what shade is it ?) " Not a pale
red."

Next object — a yellow oblong. — Agent as before. " A dusky
gold color — A square of some yellow shade."

Object — the printed letter r. — Told it was a letter ; agent as
before. " I can see R." (What sort of R ?) " An ordinary
capital R."

This illustrates feebly what often, though not always, happens
with Miss E., — that the idea of the object is grasped rather than
its actual shape.

Another object — a small printed e. — " Is it E ? " (Yes.) But,
again, she could n't tell what sort of E it was.

Object — a teapot cut out of silver paper. — Present — Dr. Herd-

ORIGINAL.   REPRODUCTION.

man, Miss R——d, and Miss R., Miss R. holding percipient's hands, but all thinking of the object. Told nothing. She said, "Something light — no color — looks like a duck — like a silver duck — something oval — head at one end and tail at the other." [This is not uncommon in ducks.] The object, being rather large, was then moved further back, so that it might be more easily grasped by the agents as a whole, but percipient persisted that it was like a duck. On being told to unbandage and draw, she drew a rude and perverted copy of the teapot, but did n't know what it was unless it was a duck. Dr. Herdman then explained that he had been thinking all the time how like a duck the original teapot was, and, in fact, had been thinking more of ducks than teapots.

Next object — a hand-mirror brought in and set up in front of Miss R——d. — No contact at first. Told nothing. She said, "Is it a color?" (No.) "No, I don't see anything." Object then shifted for Miss R. to look at herself in it, holding percipient's hand. "No, I don't get this." Gave it up. I then hid the mirror in my coat, and took it out of the room. Dr. Herdman reports that while I was away Miss E. begged to know what the object had been, but the agents refused, saying that I had evidently wished to keep it secret. Half annoyed, Miss E. said, "Oh, well, it does n't matter. I believe it was a looking-glass."

Next object — a drawing of a right-angled triangle. — No contact. — "Is it like that?" drawing a triangle with her finger. (No answer.) "It's almost like a triangle." She then drew an isosceles triangle.

Next object — a drawing of two parallel but curved lines. — No contact. — "I only see two lines," indicating two parallel lines. "Now they seem to close up."

Next object — a tetrahedron outline, rudely drawn in projection.

— "Is it another triangle?" (No answer, but I silently pass round to the agents a scribbled message, " Think of a pyramid.") Miss E. then said, "I only see a triangle," — then hastily, "Pyramids of Egypt. No, I shan't do this." Asked to draw, she only drew a triangle.

Object — a rude outline of a donkey, or other quadruped. — Still no contact at first. — "Can't get it, I am sure." I then asked the agents to leave the room, and to come in and try one by one. First Miss R——d, without contact, and then with. Next Miss R., in contact, when Miss E. said, hopelessly, "An old woman in a poke bonnet." Finally I tried as agent, alone, and Miss E. said, "It's like a donkey, but I can't see it, nor can I draw it."

C. — *Experiments with both Percipients at once.*

In addition to the experiments with single percipients, I tried a few with both percipients sitting together, hoping to learn something by comparing their different perceptions of the same object.

But, unfortunately, the experiments were not very successful; sometimes they each appeared to get different aspects or the parts of object, but never very distinct or perfect impressions. The necessity of imposing silence on the percipients, as well as on the agents, was also rather irksome, and renders the results less describable without the actual drawings.

I still think that this variation might convey something interesting if pursued under favorable circumstances. Whether greater agent-power is necessary to affect two percipients as strongly as one, or whether the blankness of mind of one percipient reacts on the other, I cannot say.

With regard to the feelings of the percipients when receiving an impression, they seem to have some sort of consciousness of the action of other minds on them; and once or twice, when not so conscious, have complained that there seemed to be "no power" or anything acting, and that they not only received no impression, but did not feel as if they were going to.

I asked Miss E. what she felt when impressions were coming freely, and she said she felt a sort of influence or thrill. They both say that several objects appear to them sometimes, but that one among them persistently recurs, and they have a feeling, when they fix upon one, that it is the right one.

Sometimes they seem quite certain that they are right. Sometimes they are very uncertain, but still right. Occasionally Miss E. has been pretty confident and yet quite wrong.

One serious failure rather depresses them, and after a success others often follow. It is because of these rather delicate psychological conditions that one cannot press the variations of an experiment as far as one would do if dealing with inert and more dependable matter. Usually the presence of a stranger spoils the phenomena, though in some cases a stranger has proved a good agent straight off.

The percipients complain of no fatigue as induced by the experiments, and I have no reason to suppose that any harm is done them. The agent, on the other hand, if very energetic, is liable to contract a headache; and Mr. Guthrie himself, who was a powerful and determined agent for a long time, now feels it wiser to refrain from acting, and conducts the experiments with great moderation.

If experiments are only conducted for an hour or so a week, no harm can, I should judge, result, and it would be very interesting to know what percentage of people have the perceptive faculty well developed.

The experiments are easy to try, but they should be tried soberly and quietly, like any other experiment. A public platform is a most unsuitable place; and nothing tried before a mixed or jovial audience can be of the slightest scientific value. Such demonstrations may be efficient in putting money into the pockets of showmen, or in amusing one's friends; but all real evidence must be obtained in the quiet of the laboratory or the study.

VIII.

MAN naturally shrinks from what appears to him to be super-natural.[1] But if man could only understand that nothing which can come within his ken can by any possibility be supernatural, all cause for shrinking must vanish. Man is but a part of Nature; beyond Nature he cannot go. Everything that occurs, and that he knows occurs, is of necessity a *natural* occurrence, something which occurs because of a natural law. Man may not know that law, but he is equipped with perceptive and rea-soning faculties, the former with which to determine whether alleged phenomena do or do not occur, and the latter with which to deduce from their study and investigation the conditions under which they occur and the laws which govern their occur-rence. To relegate any phenomena to the fanciful category of the *super*natural is to say that one is too ignorant or too dishon-est to give them the study and investigation which alone can account for, and alone have explained, all known phenomena. The savage finds it easiest to account for the tides by attributing them to supernatural causes, but patient and honest investiga-tion and comparison have shown that they result from the vary-ing attraction of the sun and moon, coupled with the rotation of the earth on its axis. To the uninstructed, the production of a current of electricity in a piece of wire by a current passing through another wire in its vicinity, but not touching it, is an inexplicable marvel; but to those who have informed themselves, while no less a marvel, it is a *natural* marvel, because they have learned that this phenomenon of induction occurs in accordance with fixed laws, which experiment, thought, comparison, and

[1] As the reader has learned, all in this book that precedes this page is compiled from the published proceedings of the London Society for Psychical Research. What follows is wholly my own, and I alone am responsible for it. — W. A. H.

study have reduced to exact form. Until we have exhausted
the possibilities of Nature, and have discovered all of Nature's
laws, — as yet we know but few of them, — let us be content to
believe that our failure to understand a thing does not necessarily involve the inability of natural law to account for it.

If no such thing as a magnet had ever been known or seen,
and a man should state on his unsupported evidence that he had
been shown a piece of iron which had the power of attracting
towards and holding to its surface, other smaller pieces of iron,
the probability is that the public would dismiss the subject with
the remark that either he had been deceived by a piece of
clever jugglery, or that he had made the story up out of the
whole cloth. In proof of this, the public would take a piece of
iron, show that it had no such power, and deduce from its experiment this conclusion : " Admitting, as a matter of argument,
that the substance *did* attract and hold pieces of iron, it is clear
that it *was not iron*, for we have tried the experiment, and *iron*
will not do it." If, undaunted by this criticism, the man should
further allege that the piece of iron which he saw do these marvellous things had the power of imparting this same power to
other pieces of iron, by mere contact with them, the public would
rise as one man and call him a fool, on the ground that any such
phenomenon was clearly contrary to the laws of matter ; for-
getting, as the public always forgets, that no man has yet
obtained a complete and authentic copy of Nature's Revised
Statutes, and that there may be, and doubtless are, between its
covers, enactments with whose provisions it is not yet familiar.
If, undaunted still, despite the charge of mental incapacity
added to that of knavery, the man should seek out the owner of
the marvellous piece of iron, apply a knife-blade to it, and, to
his own satisfaction, ascertain that the knife-blade had become
possessed of the power, he would naturally expect, on taking it to
the public and showing them its action, to have that eminent
body confess itself in the wrong. But if, unfortunately, when it
came to the test, some little time having intervened, the knife-
blade did not work, the public would deride him as a lunatic,
and his sole excuse would be that, for some reason unknown to

him, the power had waned. This the public would consider a more barefaced and ridiculous assertion than any that had gone before, and would indignantly ask whether he took them to be drivelling idiots, that he dared thus to impose upon them.

In process of time other men would appear, claiming to have seen such pieces of iron, and at length some fortunate possessor of a fragment would come to the front and offer to display its powers — *for a consideration*. To many the owner's determination to make money out of his "find" would be a new proof of fraud, and in all reasonable probability they would refuse to investigate. But some would investigate, especially if they could do so unobserved. If they saw the least loophole for possible fraud, they would loudly decry the whole thing as sheer humbug; but if, on the contrary, they saw things they could not explain according to their knowledge of Nature's laws, *they would keep very still*. At length, however, enough people of integrity and ability would pluck up courage to assert their belief that there was reasonable ground for supposing that there was, amid much delusion and deception, a certain amount of evidence going to show that such a power did reside in certain phenomenal pieces of what appeared to be iron. Having reached this conclusion, they would form a " Society for the Study of Things called Magnets, and the Alleged Phenomena therewith Connected," and then would begin a series of careful experiments by *instructed* and *capable* persons, which would result in their conviction that there did exist in nature certain pieces of a mineral substance having all the characteristics and properties of iron, which, in addition, had EXACTLY those marvellous properties described by the man who first brought the subject to the attention of the public, in return for which valuable information the public proceeded to declare its firm conviction that he was either a knave or a fool, or, more likely, both. But after the facts had been established through investigation by reputable and instructed persons, who were ridiculed for even considering them seriously — probably a long time after — the public would accept them, ignore its own action in the premises, and immediately proceed to double-lock the doors of its mind against any more intrusions from people impiously seeking to overthrow the Laws of Matter!

Why, it will be asked, are deception and fraud necessary concomitants in such cases. The reason is not far to seek or hard to find. When honest and capable men abstain from politics, because they believe politics to be corrupt and fear to be defiled, they help to make politics more corrupt by abandoning the management of politics to corrupt men. When the public puts a certain class of phenomena under the ban, and says to all, "touch them at your peril," it naturally follows that for a long time many men competent to investigate them fear to do so, and leave them chiefly in the hands of persons either uninstructed, or unscrupulous, or both. With such persons gain is the chief end, and what they cannot produce by fair means they will produce by unfair means, for their gains depend upon results, and results they must have. Hence it is that before any new truth in nature reaches the point where it receives honest investigation, it is largely left to the tender mercies of charlatans. But this does not affect or alter the original truth in any way, nor are the charlatans solely or even chiefly to be blamed. The fault rests largely with those who found it more convenient to ridicule and deny than to investigate and study. *Their dishonesty is as great as that of the charlatans, and, according to their light, far more culpable.*

In what has been said of the attitude of the public towards new truths in nature, the object has been rather to state facts than to make criticisms. The public is naturally conservative and sceptical. It is better that it is so. It would be far worse were it prone to accept everything. But there is a middle course, which is better still. This is never to deny or ridicule because one does not understand. The good woman who believed her sailor son when he said he saw the remains of Pharaoh's chariots in the Red Sea, but called him to account for lying when he said he saw flying-fish in the Pacific, is to be remembered. In front of the imperial palace in Berlin stand two bronze horses, each held by the bridle by a figure on foot. A German wit has said that they typify the government of

Bismarck — one showing "Progress Restrained," the other, "Conservatism Assisted." It may safely be said that when any new truth, in science, morals, politics, law, medicine, or any other department of human knowledge, has come up for recognition, the first thing has not been to investigate and study, but rather to deny, ridicule, and abuse. Truth always wins its way, and it is right that it should be made to prove itself by so doing. It need ask no favor; but it does seem strange that those who are chiefly to benefit by it if it be truth, and whom it cannot harm if it be other than truth, should exhaust all the resources of ingenuity and even malice in throwing obstacles in its path.

It is of the utmost importance continually to bear in mind that all phenomena which actually occur are to be accounted for by natural law, and it is also to be remembered that one should first seek to account for them by *known* natural law. When that fails, and only when that fails, is it necessary to seek further law, as yet unknown. Even if the perusal of this book has not convinced him that such a thing as mind-reading does exist in certain cases, I want the reader to admit, for the purpose of argument, that it does, because it can be shown, with reasonable certainty, to account for some things which are commonly attributed to very different causes. To this end I shall relate certain events which happened many years ago, " part of which I was, and all of which I saw." I might easily cite other cases, and for some reasons should prefer to do so, but the strength and value of this "exact relation " lies in its truth, and for that I, and others whom I shall name, can vouch.

It will be remembered that the autumn of 1857 was a period of great excitement in commercial circles. Business had been done at high pressure, loans were greatly expanded, and money commanded very high rates of interest. At length the storm burst, hundreds of business houses were wrecked, industry came to a standstill, and merchandise of all sorts, failing to find a market, fell rapidly in value. It was naturally a time of great anxiety among all business men, and those who had stood up under the storm and carried safely through looked forward with no little interest to the story which their books would tell at the end of the year. My father was then at the head of the business house which still bears his name. The firm had then, as now, a branch house in Paris, presided over by a resident partner, who bought the goods and made payments for them. There was no Atlantic cable in operation then, and, in order to enable the Boston house to make up the firm's accounts to February 1, the end of its business year, the Paris house made up its accounts to January 1, and forwarded its statement by mail, so that it would reach Boston in ample time. It was near the middle of January, 1858, that my father, one bright Sunday morning, asked my eldest brother to go to the post office and get the mail, remarking that he expected to receive a letter from the Paris house, with the account-current for the six months last past. My brother did so, and soon returned with the letters, among which was the one expected. My father opened it at the breakfast-table, took out the account-current, and expressed his satisfaction with the figures. Soon after, the whole family went up-stairs, and nothing more was thought of the matter until about an hour later, when my father's partner, Mr. E., called, with the special object of ascertaining whether the looked-for account-current had been received. My father looked through his letters for the paper, ransacked his pockets, and made a general search for the document, but it could not be found. That he had taken it with him to the library, and that he had again looked at it there, he was absolutely positive; but where it was he could not imagine. The household was called in, every possible place was searched, and some of us went even so far as to go out into the street to see if, by any chance, it had blown out of the window, which some one might possibly have opened for a moment. I remember distinctly that while I was going up-stairs on my knees, inspecting every stair thoroughly, Mr. E. remarked to me that if I found that paper it would be the best paying job I ever did, and he added something about a twenty-dollar gold piece. But, even with this stimulus, our efforts were unavailing, and finally the search was given up, and a telegram was sent to Halifax to intercept an outgoing steamer, by which the Paris house was asked to send a duplicate of the missing paper.

Three days later, while I was at work in a little attic room, which it pleased me to call my laboratory, I was called down into the parlor by my mother. I found there two ladies who had just called. One was Mrs. E., the wife of my father's partner, and the other was her sister. The doors were closed, and my mother and I were informed, in great secrecy, that Mr. E. had worried very much over the loss of the account-current, that its unaccountable disappearance had disturbed him greatly, and that they, his wife and sister-in-law, without his knowledge, had determined to consult a clairvoyant. This they did, and from this consultation they came directly to see my mother. Whether the person consulted was a man or a woman I do not remember. Who it was I never knew. Their statement was that this person, without their saying anything more than that they were seeking something lost, told them that the article in question was a paper; that it was important; that its loss was annoying; that it was without intrinsic value; that it was in a very dark place; that there was a very pungent odor of pine wood in the vicinity; and that it would be found. It immediately occurred to my mother and myself that in a closet of the library there was, in one corner, a pile of pine wood, ready for use as kindling for the library fire, and we thought it possible that, by some accident, the paper had got into or behind it. It was agreed that nothing should be said, especially to my father, but that due search should be made. Fortunately for our plans it happened that my father went out of town that day to be gone over night. Late in the evening, when the rest of the household had retired, my mother and I went to the closet in question. Stick by stick I took out every particle of that wood, and then, candle in hand, and down on my knees, I went over every inch of that floor, but no document appeared. So I put the wood back again and went to bed, feeling that I was foolish to give any heed to what clairvoyants said, and very glad indeed that no mention of the subject had been made to my father.

One week from that day my father was in his library, smoking an after-dinner cigar, and talking with Wendell Phillips, who had called for an hour's chat. I looked into the room for a moment, on my way up-stairs, and my father called to me to come in and give him the correct version of a quotation from the Biglow Papers, concerning whose exact wording he and Mr. Phillips disagreed. My version, given off-hand, was different from either, so I was set to work to hunt up the volume and settle the point. But it was missing from the book-case, and my father, turning to my mother, handed her his bunch of keys, and asked her to go to his desk, which was very seldom used, unlock it, and get out his common-place book, in which, he said, the quotation was written down. My mother did so. I, anxious to see the quotation, was standing by her side. When the desk was opened there poured out a perfect flood of the odor of pine. On the common-place book rested a cardboard box filled with patent kindlings, in the shape of compressed blocks, each about an inch square, of resin or pitch and sawdust. This box and its contents neither my mother nor myself had ever seen before. Taking the book, my mother opened it to find the quotation, and *there lay the missing paper*. My father was dumbfounded, especially as on the first day, when the general search was in progress, my mother had asked him for his keys, that she might look through the desk. He replied that it was useless, that he had not been to his desk for weeks, and that he did not want his papers disturbed.

I have not told this story for the sake of relating a marvel. My object is to show that it is capable of a solution comparatively simple. Of course the fact was that my father had, " mechanically," as we say, gone to his desk for some purpose, opened his common-place book, put the paper into it, closed, and put it down, put the box of kindlings on top of it, and then locked the desk. He had simply forgotten the circumstance absolutely. But he *knew* it, that is, *his mind* knew it. The impression was there. His brain contained all the facts in the case, *and his alone*. But, owing to a temporary lapse of memory, he failed to be cognizant of, or, as we say, to recall, things which, as a matter of fact, he knew. Now, admitting mind-reading as a possibility, we account for the statements of the "clairvoyant" by supposing that he, if it was a man, was able to read certain impressions on my father's mind better than my father could read them himself, without, however, having the least idea whose mind it was he was reading. Admitting mind-reading to have been proved to exist as a phenomenon, there is nothing marvellous, mystical, or occult about this. It is simply a natural process going on under a natural law of which as yet we know but little.

It will naturally be asked how it happened that the "clairvoyant's" mind reached and selected my father's so readily. It did not "happen" at all in the ordinary sense of the word. If the hypothesis be correct, and his mind did reach my father's, it was by a perfectly natural law, a law which we do not know. But let us see if we cannot get a hint of it. Both the ladies who called upon the clairvoyant knew, as a matter of fact, for they had been told by Mr. E., that the missing document had been in my father's hands, and that it was while in his keeping that it was lost. There is nothing to show that they *thought* of this while in the clairvoyant's presence. Whether they did or did not is immaterial. Their minds knew the fact, for it had been impressed upon their brains. Now, admitting mind-reading to be true, it is not a violent assumption to say that the clairvoyant's mind, without his knowledge, became cognizant of this impression, and then, by a law of attraction which is as yet a sealed book to us all, sought and found the mind indicated. Thus an intermediate piece of mind-reading possibly helped to pave the way for the ultimate mind-reading.

There is another hypothesis which may, to some, seem more reasonable. There is evidence which goes to show that a human mind may receive an impression unconsciously, and reflect it to another mind, also unconsciously. For instance, it is possible that the brain of Mr. E. received, all unconsciously to him, the impression which certainly was on my father's brain, but of whose existence my father was unaware. This image, unconsciously conveyed to his home by Mr. E., may have found a reflection in the brain of Mrs. E., and this reflection it was, possibly, that the clairvoyant perceived. This is not, to me, a very reasonable hypothesis, because Nature is apt to work in a very direct manner. But it has been suggested as possible. It is to be added that it is probable; — I speak now on the basis of much recorded testimony, — I say it is probable, and I might say that it is almost certain, that had that clairvoyant been brought to my parents' house, and taken to the library, my father being present, he would *at once* have gone to the writing desk to seek for the lost paper, simply because he was an expert mind-reader, and would have had little difficulty in getting at the impression on my father's brain.

In the whole range of physical experiment there is nothing more wonderful or more instructive to consider than the latent image on a photographic plate. A sheet of glass has upon its surface a film of gelatine, which carries in its substance a salt of silver, sensitive to light. When it suits our purpose we expose this, for a fractional part of a second to the light as it comes through a suitable lens, an image of the landscape for an infinitesimal period of time resting upon it. We take this plate — it may be an hour after or a year after — into a dark room, and by a faint light examine it carefully. Not the least change can we detect in it. It has the same even, creamy surface, and nothing is seen to indicate that a picture, full of intricate details, has ever rested upon its surface. But the picture, though unseen, is there. We have but to apply the proper chemicals, — *that is, establish the right conditions,* — and every detail of the landscape comes gradually out, and at length the picture is "developed." In that wonderful laboratory which we call the mind, impressions are constantly being received, and it may sometimes seem to happen that, for reasons unknown, development is deferred. *But the images are there.* Sometimes the photographer of landscapes neglects to develop his plates. They fall, perhaps, into the hands of another, whose curiosity is aroused, and he develops them. Are we not justified in believing that possibly the undeveloped and unconsciously held impression in one brain may sometimes be developed and discerned by another? This leads to the assumption that *uncon-*

scious mind-reading *may* be common; that is, that our brains *may* constantly be receiving reflections from other brains without our knowledge, and sometimes without our being cognizant of what they are after they are received. If this be true — it is only an hypothesis — we need for brain use just what every photographer needs for laboratory use — *a good developer*.

Let it not be supposed that I claim to explain all clairvoyance by the hypothesis of mind-reading, direct or indirect. To do so would be to manifest a lamentable ignorance of what clairvoyance has accomplished. I have said that it is most reasonable and best always to account for phenomena by laws whose existence we know, and whose operation we in some measure understand, when such phenomena can reasonably be so accounted for; but this not only leaves us free, — it compels us to assume the existence of some other law, to us as yet unknown, when we are confronted with phenomena for which such law as we have at least some knowledge of, will not account. When a "sensitive" sees, or thinks he sees, objects which are hidden from his physical sight, in cases where the thing seen is known, consciously or unconsciously, to another person, it may be that the impression of sight is but that produced by reflection or projection from the mind of the other person; but, in cases where the thing seen is absolutely unknown to any human being, this hypothesis is not sufficient, and we are in duty bound, as honest investigators, to seek for an hypothesis that will. For just so surely as this phenomenon can be proved to have occurred — and it most certainly can — just so sure is it that its occurrence is governed by a natural law which, by experiment, study, and thought, we shall in time get at.

Some may be curious to ask what thing can exist whose existence is unknown to any human being, so that its discovery by clairvoyance would be a phenomenon coming under the second head. There may be many, but it will be sufficient to say that there have been cases where persons claimed, by clairvoyance, to be cognizant of what was going on inside of human bodies, giving correct diagnoses of obscure and unsuspected difficulties, which, on proper examination, were proved to exist, although their existence was stoutly denied, because not believed by the patient. In some cases the statements made by such "clairvoyants" have been disbelieved and ridiculed until after death, when the dissecting-knife has proved their truth. Let it not be supposed from this that I believe such a power at all common, or that any considerable number of those who claim it really possess it. On the contrary, it is just in this line that many charlatans practise upon the ignorance and credulity of the public. What I do say is, that such such cases have occurred, that they are too exact and precise in their details to be classed as coincidences, and that they challenge and justly claim investigation, to the end that this faculty may be used for the good of mankind, and that those who falsely claim to possess it may be branded as impostors, and the public put on their guard against them.

It is to be observed that there are two distinct phases of mind-reading, into which all cases divide themselves. In the one the agent, or person whose mind is read, is active, seeking to concentrate his thoughts, and making an effort of the will to project them upon the mind of the percipient, who is simply seeking to be passive and receptive. In the other it is the percipient whose mind is active. His mind is seeking for, and striving to get at, what is in the mind of the agent, who is entirely passive. Moreover, whatever his *mind* may know about it, he is generally unconscious that any effort is being made by another mind to learn what his contains. I say "generally," because some persons, extremely sensitive, say that a peculiar feeling comes over them when a percipient is seeking, even at a distance, to obtain an impression of their thoughts.

It is a question whether mind-reading, in all its forms and phases, — mesmerism, clairvoyance, and other allied phenomena bearing names which have no place in scientific nomenclature, — are not all, like static, magnetic, and galvanic electricity, different forms of the same force. They have been named haphazard, and phenomena are classed under these arbitrary heads according to the inclination and knowledge of different experimenters. It is certain that they are closely allied, just as it is certain that they overlap one another, so that there is no clearly defined line of demarcation between them, and it is not altogether improbable that when, by sufficient study, we have mastered them, we shall find that they all exist under the operation of one great natural law.

There are those who deny the reality of mesmerism or hypnotism. They are uninstructed persons, — uninstructed in this matter, I mean. Their denial is unimportant to those who have studied the subject, and their opinion, based on ignorance, is as valueless as mine on the question of a Sanskrit root. To those who have taken the pains to inform themselves, experiment for the purpose of establishing *the fact* of mesmerism is as needless as for physicians to cut up the living body to establish the known fact that the blood circulates. Experiment for the purpose of studying the phenomenon they consider of the highest value, but, so far as the fact is concerned, they do not need to waste time to learn what they absolutely know. With the long array of recorded experiments which the books contain, experiments conducted by men of known ability and unquestioned integrity, it seems like " wasteful and ridiculous excess " to cite cases that have come under my own eye ; but I may briefly say, that on one occasion, when I half suspected that the " subject " was pretending to think that the liquid which I gave him to smell was cologne, when it was really water, I substituted strong aqua ammonia, telling him, as before, that it was cologne. He drenched his handkerchief in it, and held it to his nostrils, apparently with great satisfaction. I know that what little of the fumes came to mine brought water to my eyes, and gave me a choking sensation, and I was convinced that in suspecting him of shamming I had done him a great injustice. After experiences such as this, insignificant compared with the mass of recorded testimony from authorities which no fair-minded man can question, if he will but take the pains to examine it, — no one can deny the reality of mesmerism any more than he can deny that water is the result of the chemical combination of oxygen and hydrogen, a fact universally admitted, but which comparatively. few have ever seen experimentally demonstrated. They believe it to be true because its truth has been certified to them by competent authority. An examination of the records will show that the truth of the phenomena of mesmerism have been certified to by authority which, to my mind, is amply competent, and among instructed persons it is a matter of common knowledge.

It will naturally be asked what good is expected to grow out of the study of these so-called " occult " phenomena. The general answer is that nothing but good can come out of the study of nature. It is something to free men's minds from delusion as to the supernatural. It is the province of man to study Nature in all her moods and phases, and discover her laws. The special answer in the case of mesmerism is that it is a phenomenon of the mind, the least understood and most important factor in man's personality. In countless well-authenticated cases it has done important medical service by enabling the physician to reach the body through the brain, and it is held by many persons of wide acquaintance with the subject that it contains the key to the correct understanding and treatment of the most terrible of all diseases, insanity. But before it can be safely used, it must be closely and exhaustively studied, lest by wrong use, like all true remedies, it do more harm than good. If it be objected that only comparatively few persons can be influenced in this way, and that it is senseless to study out the proper use of a force or remedy which can only be used in rare and exceptional cases, the answer is that, until we know much more about it than is now known, we are *not* in a position to say how widely it may or may not be used. There is reason to believe that more or less of what is, to say the least, closely allied to mesmerism, is practised very generally all the time, for the most part unconsciously, and for all sorts of purposes. Is it not worth the study to ascertain just what this is, both that it may be used for proper purposes, and that those more or less subject to such influences may know how to detect and guard against them when they are used, even unconsciously, for purposes not proper; that is, where a person is induced, by what we call superior will-power, to do a thing which he knows perfectly well it is not for his interest to do.

I mention this unconscious use of mesmeric influence because I believe it to be far more frequent than is generally supposed; far more frequent, indeed, than its conscious or even intentional use. A case in point came within my experience not long since. A travelling salesman, a "drummer," was seeking to sell certain goods to a customer. His arguments were by no means potent, his command of language was very limited, but he was an earnest man, and, saying the same thing over and over again, kept his eyes fixed on his customer. The latter at first declined to purchase, but the drummer clung to him. What he said was not enough in itself to have any effect, but his manner, his earnestness, and, above all, his fixed gaze, did the business in time. The customer simply wilted, and consented. Now there was nothing remarkable in this. It happens every day; but I, who have become somewhat familiar with the appearance of subjects when partially or wholly under mesmeric influence, felt convinced that I recognized it in the case of this customer. The expression of his face, especially about the eyes, changed completely; he grew nervous and uneasy, and when he finally consented to take the goods, it was as though he realized that he did not need them, and that he took them to rid himself of his tormentor. Is it not barely possible that it will pay to investigate mesmerism and all of its belongings, if for no other purpose than to ascertain what can be done to resist such influences?

A clergyman of the Church of England recently told me that once, when the community in which he then resided had been greatly disturbed by the circulation of a pamphlet by Bradlaugh, in which it was asserted that man had no soul, he temporarily added to the consternation by preaching a sermon in which he coincided with Bradlaugh's statement, adding, however, by way of explanation, that the soul and the man were identical, and that while it was true that the man, or the soul, whichever you choose to call it, had a body, it was an absurd confusion of terms to say that man, who was nothing if not a soul, had a soul. Of course it was in one sense a play upon words, but to my mind a justifiable one. We all *know* that the body dies. Pretty nearly all of us believe that the entity which we call the

soul or the spirit — in a word, *the man himself* — does not die. We
believe that, when the body dies, dissolution takes place, that is,
that the soul, or the spirit, or the man himself, is freed from the
body and continues to live as an entity.   There is nothing startling, nothing new, nothing surprising in this belief.   It is taught
in every family circle, in every Sunday school, in every church
of every Christian sect throughout the whole civilized world.   It
is the belief of by far the greater part of what we presume to
call the uncivilized world.   It is the basis of Christian hope and
Christian faith, and to the minds of the vast majority of mankind it appears reasonable and natural.   I have been careful to
say that while we *know* the death of the body to be actual, we
can only say that we *believe* the life of the individual to continue.
But this belief is so strong that it may be assumed as a fact, at
least for purposes of argument.   We are further taught that when
the spirit (we may as well call the disembodied personality by
this commonly accepted term, understanding that it includes all
that there is of a man save the material body) leaves the body,
it *ascends*.   It is hardly to be supposed that, in this enlightened
age, this statement is to be taken literally in the sense of an
upward movement, a movement in a direction opposite to that
in which the centre of the earth lies.   Any such literal construc-
tion would imply that the thousands of spirits which are daily
released from the bodies which they have inhabited go sailing
off into endless space on divergent lines, *never to meet*.   Clearly
the literal interpretation will not do.   It is more reasonable to
suppose that, in saying that, the spirit on being released *ascends*,
we mean that it passes to a higher state, a better, freer, and
more untrammelled condition, — in a word, that it enters upon
and is born into that state of existence that we call "spiritual."
To suppose that it ceases to have thought is revolting.   To suppose that man, on passing out of his body, ceases to have any
memory of mundane things, is not absolutely repugnant to any
facts within common knowledge, but it is not a pleasant idea to
contemplate.   If, when dissolution takes place, all that experience has taught him, all the affections that he has formed, all
the friends that he has made, all the hopes and aspirations of

his heart for those near and dear to him, are to be blotted from his memory, what will he be, what can he be, but a hopeless disappointment to those he leaves behind, when their time comes and they join him? Nay, if all antecedent recollection is to be blotted from the pages of *their* memory likewise, if all their affections and friendships die when their bodies die, they must meet as strangers those who went before, to whom during existence in the body they were bound by the closest ties of love and friendship. This is hardly the proposition to put before the mother who has lost her child, the wife who has lost her husband. No, if we are to assume that all that there is of man save his body lives after dissolution, we are forced, as it seems to me, to assume that he carries with him all his knowledge, all his experience, all his thought, — in a word, all his recollection.

And now comes the great question, Can man, having passed from the body, and entered upon a new phase of existence, communicate his thoughts to those who yet remain in the body, and receive impressions from them. This is the question of questions, that which hundreds of thousands of human minds are to-day considering, which many have solved to their own satisfaction, — some in one way and some in another. I do not presume to solve it, but it may be a help to others, as it has been to me, to consider certain suggestions which have the merit of being simple, and which not a few have thought reasonable. The first question which comes up for consideration is, "Where are these disembodied spirits?" We do not know. Education and common belief leads us to locate them "in heaven above," but this phrase, except it be taken figuratively, conveys no clear idea of locality. In fact it means, taken literally, *everywhere except on this planet*. Now in cases where we have no exact information I take it that the most reasonable assumption is to be preferred ; and to my mind the most reasonable assumption is that the spirits of those who have ceased to inhabit earthly bodies are right here. It does not follow from this, necessarily, that they can see us or our surroundings, any more than we can see them or their surroundings. Nay, it does not even follow that they are aware even of our presence in any way. It may be that in some way not known we sometimes *sense* their presence, without the aid of either eye or ear, or any of our physical organs of sensation, and just so it may be that they sometimes sense our presence, even though possessing no material organs of sensation. I speak of these things as possibilities only, but to me they appear not unreasonable possibilities. Where these spirits are, whether they are all assembled together, or whether they are dispersed through space, is entirely immaterial to the argument. It is a matter of secondary importance altogether.

Admitting that one human mind, in the body, can in certain cases so project its thoughts as to impress them upon another human mind, also in the body — and this, upon the evidence submitted in this volume I confidently assert — it does not to me seem a violent assumption to say that the disembodied mind, possessing everything that it ever had except the body, can in certain cases project its thoughts upon minds still in the body, — in other words, impress it with ideas and thoughts foreign to itself. I cannot see why a human mind possessing this power while in the body — a power purely mental — should not possess it to even a greater degree when the body is cast aside, and all the duties which the body imposes upon the mind are things of the past, leaving it comparatively untrammelled. So long as what we call life lasts, the mind must take cognizance of every impression which comes to it through the various organs of sensation. These come in endless succession from the instant of birth to the instant of dissolution, and they supply the mind with continuous occupation. But when the body dies, these sensations cease to occupy the mind's attention, *it has so much the less to do*, and consequently it is more free to engage in operations purely mental, and among these *may be* thought-projection upon other minds, *embodied or disembodied.*

Let us now come back to a suggestion which I have made many times in the course of this chapter, but which cannot be too often repeated, If the embodied mind can, in certain cases, communicate and project its thoughts upon another human mind, — and I assert that it can, — it does so by virtue of and under a natural law. In the same way, if the disembodied mind can communicate and project its thoughts upon the embodied mind — I have offered no proof of this, and hence do not assert it — it does it under the same law, for the mind no longer in the body is as much a part of Nature as ever, — it cannot pass beyond Nature. Hence such thought projection or impression is not in any sense *super*natural, it is nothing to be shunned, it is nothing to be feared. If it occurs — and this is yet to be proved — it is a most important, valuable, attractive, and interesting thing to investigate. To say that it does not admit of investigation is absurd.

I have already exceeded the limits prescribed for this volume. I have given in detail the most authentic and reliable evidence attainable concerning the existence of mind-reading, and I submit that it is sufficient to establish it as a fact. I have touched upon mesmerism, clairvoyance, and other phenomena which lie "beyond" mind-reading, and have thus, at least in part, redeemed the promise of my book's title. Concerning these there are many proofs to be adduced, much argument to be submitted. These I shall hope to present in a later volume. Meantime I ask the reader to entertain no proposition that does not appeal to his reason, to believe nothing that is not proved, and at the same time I ask him to banish all prejudice from his mind, and to remember that superstition is, and always has been, a stumbling-block in the path of human progress.

As an investigator anxious to learn from the experience of others, I ask that any of my readers who have within their knowledge well-authenticated cases of the occurrence of any of these phenomena will, if they find it agreeable and convenient, communicate them to me. It is not necessary that the names of all the parties concerned be given, although, where there is no objection, that is immensely preferable. What is absolutely essential is that the facts be attested by the full name and address of one or more persons who know them of their own knowledge. Any such communication will reach me most speedily if sent to the care of the publishers of this volume, Messrs. Lee and Shepard, Boston.

LEE AND SHEPARD'S HANDBOOKS.

"JUST AS THE TWIG IS BENT, THE TREE'S INCLINED."

LESSONS ON MANNERS. For home and school use. A Manual by EDITH E. WIGGIN. Cloth, 50 cents ; school edition, boards, 30 cents net.

This little book is being rapidly introduced into schools as a text-book.

SHOWS WHY THE WINDS BLOW.

WHIRLWINDS, CYCLONES, AND TORNADOES. By Prof. W. M. DAVIS of Harvard University. Illustrated. 50 cents.

The cyclones of our great West, the whirlwinds of the desert, every thing in the shape of storms, scientifically and popularly treated.

"THIS VOLUME IS SUBLIME POETRY."

THE STARS AND THE EARTH; or, Thoughts upon Space, Time, and Eternity. With an Introduction by THOMAS HILL, D.D., LL.D., late President of Harvard University. Cloth. 50 cents.

" It cannot but be valuable to the student of science as well as to the professors of religion, and tends to bring them closer together, and reconcile them." — *Potter's Monthly.*

KNOW WHAT YOU ARE DRINKING.

HAND BOOK OF WATER ANALYSIS. By Dr. GEORGE L. AUSTIN. Cloth. 50 cents.

" It condenses into fifty pages what one would have to wander through a small chemical library to find. We commend the book as worthy of a wide circulation." — *Independent.*

EVERY LADY HER OWN FLORIST.

THE PARLOR GARDENER. A Treatise on the House-Culture of Ornamental Plants. Translated from the French, and adapted to American use. By CORNELIA J. RANDOLPH. With eleven illustrative cuts. 50 cents.

It contains minute directions for the " mantel-piece garden," the " étagère garden," the " flower-stand garden," the " portable greenhouse," the " house-aquarium," the garden upon the balcony, the terrace, and the double window, besides describing many curious and interesting experiments in grafting.

"HELLO, CENTRAL!"

THE TELEPHONE. An Account of the Phenomena of Electricity, Magnetism, and Sound, as involved in its action, with directions for making a Speaking-Telephone. By Professor A. E. DOLBEAR of Tufts College. 16mo. Illustrated. Price 50 cents.

" An interesting little book upon this most fascinating subject, which is treated in a very clear and methodical way. First we have a thorough review of the discoveries in electricity, then of magnetism, then of those in the study of sound, — pitch, velocity, timbre, tone, resonance, sympathetic vibrations, etc. From these the telephone is reached, and by them in a measure explained." — *Hartford Courant.*

Sold by all booksellers, and sent by mail, postpaid, on receipt of price.

LEE & SHEPARD, Publishers, Boston.

www.ingramcontent.com/pod-product-compliance
Lightning Source LLC
Chambersburg PA
CBHW061153120626
46546CB00005B/2042

* 9 7 8 1 9 5 8 6 0 4 1 5 1 *